RIVER RUNNERS'
GUIDE TO Utah
and adjacent areas

RIVER RUNNERS' GUIDE TO Utah
and adjacent areas

Revised Edition and Updated

Gary C. Nichols

The University of Utah Press
Salt Lake City

LIBRARY OF CONGRESS CATALOGING-IN-PUBLICATION DATA

Nichols, Gary C.
  River runners' guide to Utah and adjacent areas / Gary C. Nichols.—Rev. ed.
  p. cm.
  ISBN 978-0–87480–725–7 (pbk. : alk. paper)
  1. Canoes and canoeing—Utah—Guidebooks. 2. Rafting (Sports)—Utah—
Guidebooks. 3. Utah—Guidebooks. I. Title.
GV776.U8 N52 2002
917.9204'34—dc21   2001008554

14 13 12 11 10
5 4 3 2

All photographs by Gary C. Nichols unless otherwise noted.

ACKNOWLEDGMENTS

Thanks to the Giddings family, Les Jones, and Werner Huck for their help in the history section of the book. Thanks to Igage here in Salt Lake City and National Geographic for their computer programs that helped me with mapping and measuring distances.

I am also very grateful to my wife and children, who have accompanied me on some of these rivers and put up with my wanderings on others.

I could not have done many of these runs without friends who joined me, especially on exploratory runs. So thanks to Lane Johnson, Kirk Nichols, Alan James, David Gibson, Dave Hildebrand, John Keyser, Mark White, Mark Freed, Roy Piskadlo, Rod Huck, Bob Cooper, Rob Burton, Amir Stark, Jared Cieslewicz, Ed Gertler, Neil Kahn, and any others my waterlogged mind is forgetting. Thanks to Jim Howells and his buddies, who helped form the Virgin River Runners Coalition, both for their information and their untiring efforts to keep the Virgin River open to paddlers.

Finally, thanks to all who love and protect rivers, especially those who put in huge amounts of time running the organizations that help protect and keep access open to all rivers. Please support and join them.

CONTENTS

CAUTION

River running can be dangerous. Degrees of difficulty are at best subjective assessments, and conditions can alter with changes in water level, seasons of the year, equipment used, and experience of the river runner. Part of the beauty of running rivers is that they are a fluid medium. They are never exactly the same from moment to moment. A run one day will vary slightly from one the next day. Natural and human events can radically alter a section of river. A flash flood can turn a Class 2 rapid into a Class 5 in minutes. A channel can be clear one day and blocked with trees the next day. Flow levels can dramatically change the character of a river. Man can alter the flow, block the river, or change its course. We recommend that you receive proper instruction from a qualified person or organization. Then start with easy rivers and build up the skills necessary to handle harder runs. Use proper equipment. Do all you can to find out about any changes in a run since this book was published. A guidebook can give you only a rough idea of what to expect at a given time. Guidebooks are no substitute for good judgment.

The author and publisher are not responsible for how you use this book, how you maintain personal safety, or the decisions you make on running a river or a particular rapid. Only you are responsible. You assume this responsibility when you choose to go on a river.

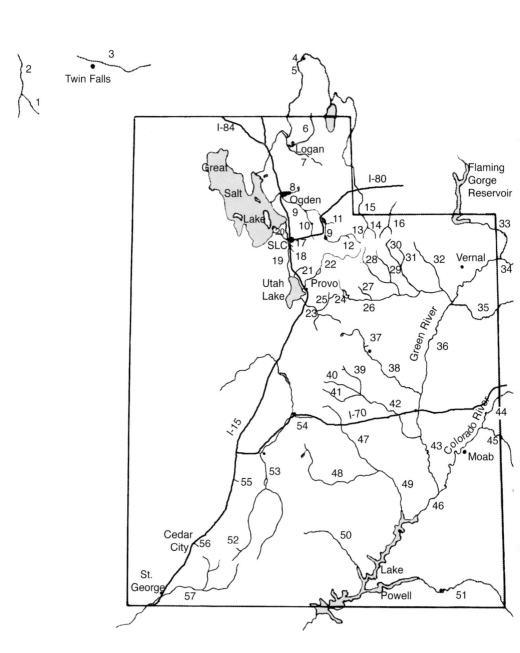

2

3
Twin Falls

1

I-84

4
5

6

Logan
7

Great
Salt
Lake

I-80

Flaming
Gorge
Reservoir

15

8
Ogden
9

11

33

10

20

9

SLC
17

18

19

21

22

Utah
Lake

Provo

25

24

23

13 14 16

12

28

30

31 32 Vernal

29

27

26

34

35

Green River

36

37

39

38

40

41

42

I-70

54

47

I-15

53

55

48

56 52

Cedar
City

St.
George
57

50

Lake

Powell

46

49

43

Colorado River

44

45

Moab

51

KEY TO RIVERS ON UTAH MAP

1. Jarbidge River
2. Bruneau River
3. Snake River
4. Black Canyon of the Bear
5. Oneida Narrows of the Bear
6. Logan River
7. Blacksmith Fork
8. Ogden River
9. Weber River
10. East Canyon Creek
11. Chalk Creek
12. Smith & Morehouse Creek
13. Hayden Fork of the Bear
14. East Fork of the Bear
15. Bear River
16. Blacks Fork
17. Big Cottonwood Creek
18. Little Cottonwood Creek
19. Jordan River
20. Surplus Canal for Jordan River
21. American Fork
22. Provo River
23. Spanish Fork River
24. Sixth Water
25. Diamond Fork
26. Strawberry River
27. Currant Creek
28. Duchesne River
29. Rock Creek
30. Lake Fork
31. Yellowstone River
32. Uinta River
33. Lodore Canyon of the Green River
34. Yampa River
35. White River
36. Desolation Canyon of the Green River
37. Willow Creek
38. Price River
39. Huntington Creek
40. Cottonwood Creek
41. Ferron Creek
42. San Rafael River
43. Labyrinth Canyon of the Green River
44. Westwater Canyon of the Colorado River
45. Dolores River
46. Cataract Canyon of the Colorado River
47. Muddy Creek
48. Fremont River
49. Dirty Devil River
50. Escalante River
51. San Juan River
52. Mammoth Creek
53. Sevier River
54. Salina Creek
55. Beaver Creek
56. Coal Creek
57. Virgin River

It has been 15 years since the last edition of this book was written. It's way past time to redo it. Many changes have taken place, and I have been able to run a number of new rivers. So I decided to start from scratch and rewrite the book, not just revise parts. Most of the rivers I have rerun. Unfortunately, that takes several years. So some of the information in this book is already a couple of years old.

Utah is still the second driest state in the country, but that doesn't mean there aren't lots of river running possibilities. I'm amazed at how many rivers there are. It does mean that the season is short, though, on most rivers. There are rivers for every level of boater from the total beginner to the most skilled. A list, broken down by difficulty, is available at the back of the book. There are rivers for every type of craft. I haven't listed what type of craft to use because that depends on your ability and the size of your craft. Generally, though, if the **Character** section lists the river as being small and steep, you will have a tough time getting a raft down it. Also, look at the flow. If it's a low-volume river (below about 500 cfs) you'll find getting a raft down it also a challenge. The large rivers are raftable, but the majority of the rivers in the state are small. They are best run in kayaks or inflatable kayaks and sometimes canoes. Open canoeists will usually want extra flotation in their canoes if there are rapids. Most general-purpose canoes will get destroyed in the small, steep, technical rivers. Short, highly rockered whitewater canoes in skilled hands can handle any of the runs that kayakers go on.

I have again included a few rivers outside Utah. They are rivers that are fairly close and often flow into or out of Utah or are a tributary of a river that goes into Utah.

The rivers are listed alphabetically for ease of reference if you already know their names. If you are going to a certain area and want to know what rivers are near there, look at the Utah map at the beginning of the book to find the names of the rivers and then look up the description.

Staying within your ability is one of the keys to safe river running. Each section is rated according to the International Scale of River **Difficulty** where Class 1 is the easiest and Class 6 is the hardest. See the back of the book for details of this scale. A (P) means there is at least one portage. Be advised that all rivers have potential portages due to logs or other shifting hazards, or to your own skill level. Know your ability. If you don't, start out on something easy and see where you fit in with the ratings in this book. Ratings are subjective and vary at different flow levels. The ratings in this book are just general guidelines. You must make your own decisions as to whether you can run a rapid or not. When in doubt, scout. Trust your gut feelings. If you don't feel good about a run, walk. You can always come back another time and run it. If you die, you can't.

A **time** is listed for each run. This can really vary depending on your purpose for being there. I've listed what I think is an average range. Your time could be quite different.

One of the bigger challenges to running a new river is knowing where to get in and out. Quite a bit of space has been devoted to **access**. Hopefully, between the text and the maps, you won't have any trouble. Access points do change occasionally. Sometimes this is because of private property. Most of the access points listed are on public land. Occasionally, though, the land ownership is not known. Being friendly and courteous goes a long way toward keeping access open. Demanding your rights, being rude, littering, making lots of noise are all ways to get an area closed.

USGS quad **maps** (7½-minute) have been listed. These will give you the most detail of the area. A less detailed map has been printed in the book for each river. This should help you with access and knowing roughly where you are. Many of the runs can be done with just the information in the book. But, personally, I like having the most detailed maps with me in case I want to hike or need to get out in an emergency. In addition, you may want to get a Utah road map to get the broad picture.

The major rivers in Utah require a **permit**. These can be tough to get and require applying way in advance—usually by the end of January. Each section lists if permits are necessary and where to apply. Good luck! Taking care of the rivers you go on helps keep restrictions such as permits down.

SAFETY

When using this guide or any other, be aware that rivers change and that varying flow levels create great differences. A guidebook can be accurate in only a general way. There is no way to list every possible hazard that you might come across. For these reasons, we do not assume responsibility for inaccuracies or omissions.

Learn all you can about any river you are considering running. Hopefully this guide will be a major factor in doing that. Check flow levels. Talk to river runners getting off a river. If commercial companies run a river, they are a great source of information, as they are often on it every day or week. Government agencies that manage the area can often be a good source of information.

Be prepared for emergencies. Have the knowledge and gear to hike out if necessary. That means knowing where you are and where access roads are. Cell phones are occasionally useful, but often the areas are too remote. Carry plenty of water or a means to purify the river water. Many of the rivers are so silty that a filter will be plugged very quickly. All rivers are suspect in regard to the water being safe to drink. Even clear ones usually have microscopic organisms such as bacteria, Giardia, and Cryptosporidium that can make you sick. Some are also very salty or high in minerals or fertilizers or other things that are not good for you. So carry water when you can.

I recommend first-aid and CPR training, especially if you're planning trips away from roads and civilization. Much of Utah has rattlesnakes, black widow spiders, and scorpions. Poison ivy is fairly common along rivers. Be careful and know how to deal with these dangers. Carry a good first-aid kit.

Learn the basic skills of boating and stay within your ability. Take a class in the type of boating you want to do whether it's kayaking, canoeing, or rafting. Take a river rescue class. Carry a throw rope and other rescue gear. There is much you can learn from books, but hands-on experience in a class is far better. If you're not aware of any classes, try calling the nearest university or college or the Red Cross.

Be sure you have adequate flotation—in the boat and on yourself. Rafts should have at least 3 separate air chambers, preferably 4. Use good equipment designed for running rivers and make sure there is nothing to get tangled in. Make sure helmets and PFDs are not only on, but also fitted properly and snug. Dress for the worst. Wet suits or dry suits can save your life in a long cold swim.

WILDERNESS ETIQUETTE

One of the nicest aspects of river running is that you can get into some remote places and you don't even leave footprints. You will, however, have some impact on access points and campsites. Desert environments are especially fragile. Decomposition is slow and it is much harder for plants to grow back after being damaged. You can minimize your impacts with some careful thought and action. If you don't do this, you will cause all of us to face closures or greater restrictions.

NOLS (National Outdoor Leadership School), the Bureau of Land Management, and the U.S. Forest Service teamed up to create the Leave No Trace program in 1991. Today, the nonprofit Leave No Trace, Inc., manages this program in conjunction with four federal land-management agencies. They have come up with seven principles of Leave No Trace that we should follow.

Plan ahead and prepare.
– Know the regulations and special concerns for the area you'll visit.
– Prepare for extreme weather, hazards, and emergencies.
– Schedule your trip to avoid times of high use.
– Visit in small groups. Split larger parties into groups of 4 to 6.
– Repackage food to minimize waste.
– Use a map and compass to eliminate the use of marking paint, rock cairns, or flagging.

Travel and camp on durable surfaces.
– Durable surfaces include established trails and campsites, rock, gravel, dry grasses, or snow.
– Protect riparian areas by camping at least 200 feet from lakes and streams.
– Good campsites are found, not made. Altering a site is not necessary.
    In popular areas:
– Concentrate use on existing trails and campsites.
– Walk single file in the middle of the trail, even when it is wet or muddy.
– Keep campsites small. Focus activity in areas where vegetation is absent.
    In pristine areas:
– Disperse use to prevent the creation of campsites and trails.
– Avoid places where impacts are just beginning.

Dispose of Waste Properly.
– Pack it in, pack it out. Inspect your campsite and rest areas for trash or spilled foods. Pack out all trash, leftover food, and litter.

- Deposit solid human waste in catholes dug 6 to 8 inches deep at least 200 feet from water, camp, and trails. Cover and disguise the cathole when finished.
- Pack out toilet paper and hygiene products.
- To wash yourself or your dishes, carry water 200 feet away from streams or lakes and use small amounts of biodegradable soap. Scatter strained dishwater.

Leave What You Find.
- Preserve the past: examine, but do not touch, cultural or historic structures and artifacts.
- Leave rocks, plants, and other natural objects as you find them.
- Avoid introducing or transporting non-native species.
- Do not build structures or furniture, or dig trenches.

Minimize Campfire Impacts.
- Campfires can cause lasting impacts to the backcountry. Use a lightweight stove for cooking and enjoy a candle lantern for light.
- Where fires are permitted, use established fire rings, fire pans, or mound fires.
- Keep fires small. Only use sticks from the ground that can be broken by hand.
- Burn all wood and coals to ash, put out campfires completely, then scatter cool ashes.

Respect Wildlife.
- Observe wildlife from a distance. Do not follow or approach them.
- Never feed animals. Feeding wildlife damages their health, alters natural behaviors, and exposes them to predators and other dangers.
- Protect wildlife and your food by storing rations and trash securely.
- Control pets at all times, or leave them at home.
- Avoid wildlife during sensitive times: mating, nesting, raising young, or winter.

Be Considerate of Other Visitors.
- Respect other visitors and protect the quality of their experience.
- Be courteous. Yield to other users on the trail.
- Step to the downhill side of the trail when encountering pack stock.

– Take breaks and camp away from trails and other visitors.
– Let nature's sounds prevail. Avoid loud voices and noises.
   These principles are geared a little more toward backpacking. For river runners we might add the following:
– Carry out all human waste and toilet paper. This is required on permitted rivers.
– When passing fishermen, try to minimize any interference by giving them a wide berth.
– Those in an eddy or playing on a wave should yield to boats coming downstream.

RIVER ORGANIZATIONS

There are several organizations that all river runners should consider joining. By joining an organization that has the same goals you do, you will be able to accomplish things that you can't easily do on your own. You gain the power of numbers and the skills of full-time people. These groups help support river running, preserve rivers, fight for access, educate, and promote safety.

ACA—American Canoe Association
1340 Central Park Blvd., Suite 210
Fredericksburg, VA 22401
Phone: 540-907-4460
Fax: 888-229-3792
http://www.americancanoe.org

AWA—American Whitewater Affiliation
http://www.americanwhitewater.org

Idaho Rivers United
P.O. Box 633
Boise, ID 83701
(208) 343-7481
http://www.idahorivers.org

Southern Utah Wilderness Alliance
425 East 100 South
Salt Lake City, UT 84111
(801) 486-3161
http://www.suwa.org

Utah Rivers Council
1055 East 2100 South, Suite 207
Salt Lake City, UT 84106
(801) 486-4776
http://www.utahrivers.org

Utah Whitewater Club
http://www.utahwhitewaterclub.org

Virgin River Runners Coalition
http://www.virginriver.org

Wasatch Mountain Club
1390 S. 1100 East, Suite 103
Salt Lake City, UT 84105
(801) 463-9842
http://www.wasatchmountainclub.org

RIVER FLOWS

Each river has a **levels** section listing the minimum flow. This is usually not the ideal level but is marginally doable. Flow information can be obtained by calling (801) 539-1311 or at http://www.cbrfc.noaa.gov, or for the whole country http://waterdata.usgs.gov/nwis/rt. Many of the organizations listed above also have links to flow information.

JORDAN RIVER
BIG & LITTLE COTTONWOOD CREEKS
AMERICAN FORK RIVER

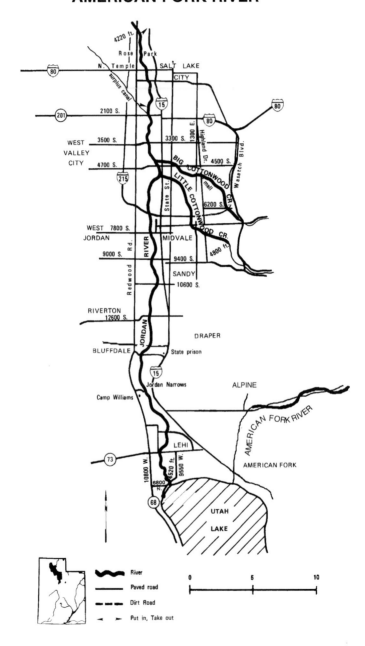

Difficulty: Class 3 to 4+ (P).
Length: 5 miles.
Average Gradient: 200 ft./mi.
Season: May, June.
Time: 3 hours.
Character: Steep, fast, narrow, rocky, logs, diversion dams.
Levels: 250 cfs to 400 cfs.
Elevation: Put-in 6100 ft., take-out 5040 ft.
Topo Maps: Timpanogos Cave, Lehi.
Permits: No.
Shuttle Length: Same as run.
Access: From I-15 take the Alpine exit and follow U-80 into American
    Fork Canyon. The road follows the river. Get in and out wherever
    you want.

This is a steep and dangerous river due to logs with almost no place to
stop above them. I would recommend scouting all the steep parts in advance. High water is probably suicidal unless you remove all the logs
beforehand. Mark White and Jeff McFarland are the only ones I know
who have run it. They did it at a medium low level and found it to be fun
and exciting. The 5-mile length listed above is from the Tibble Fork turnoff to the diversion dam at the mouth of the canyon. Below Timpanogos
Cave National Monument is a hydro-electric plant that is best portaged
on the left. There has been some discussion about removing this old
plant, which would make boating a little better.

NORTH SLOPE UINTA MOUNTAINS

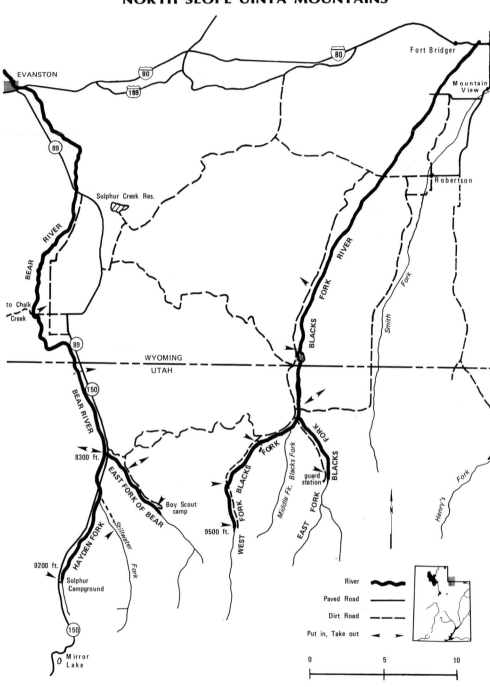

EVANSTON

Fort Bridger

Mountain View

Robertson

Sulphur Creek Res.

BEAR RIVER

to Chalk Creek

WYOMING

UTAH

BLACKS FORK RIVER

Smith Fork

BEAR RIVER

8300 ft.

EAST FORK OF BEAR

Boy Scout camp

WEST FORK BLACKS FORK

Middle Fk. Blacks Fork

EAST FORK BLACKS FORK

guard station

Henry's Fork

Stillwater Fork

9500 ft.

HAYDEN FORK

9200 ft.

Sulphur Campground

Mirror Lake

River

Paved Road

Dirt Road

Put in, Take out

0   5   10

≈ ≈ ≈ BEAR RIVER

The Bear River starts high in the Uinta Mountains in Utah, winds through Wyoming and Idaho, and returns to Utah, ending in the Great Salt Lake after traveling over 400 river miles but only 65 miles "as the crow flies." This book covers most of the whitewater stretches. An excellent book (if you can find it) for the rest of the river is *Boating the Bear,* published by the Bridgerland Audubon Society in Logan.

EAST FORK OF THE BEAR

Difficulty: Class 2 to 3+.
Length: 5 miles.
Average Gradient: 95 ft./mi.
Season: >June<.
Time: 1.5 to 3 hours.
Character: Small, narrow, tree hazards, small boulders, few eddies.
Levels: 200–400 cfs; gauge is 4.1 miles above confluence with Bear River.
Elevation: Put-in 8800 ft., take-out 8300 ft.
Topo Maps: Christmas Meadows, Deadman Mountain.
Permits: No.
Shuttle Length: 6.5 miles.
Access: Take Highway 150 from Kamas, UT, or Evanston, WY. About 10 miles south of the Utah/Wyoming line is the East Fork of the Bear River. Just north is the East Fork Campground. This is the take-out. For the put-in, go north one quarter mile and take a good dirt road east for about 2 miles and turn right on the road going to the Boy Scout camp. Put in anywhere along this road where you are close to the river.

It's best to avoid the Scout camp by putting in below it. So don't go more than about 2 miles above where you first come to the river. At first the river winds through a fairly open area with Class 1 white-water and an occasional tight turn or downed tree to avoid. This is a good warm-up in a beautiful area. When you get to about where the dirt road first came to the river, the speed picks up and you enter a small gorge. The next 2.5 miles are the hardest part, with some long continuous sections of up to Class 3 rapids. Blind turns can hide fallen trees, so proceed carefully. Depending on trees, Class 4 skills may be required. When you get to a footbridge, there is a half mile left to the confluence with the Bear River. Then you have a couple hundred yards to the campground and take-out.

HAYDEN FORK OF THE BEAR

Difficulty: Class 1 to 3.
Length: 12 miles.
Average Gradient: 65 ft./mi.
Season: >June<.
Time: 3 to 6 hours.
Character: Small, narrow, tree hazards, small boulders, few eddies in steep sections.
Levels: 200 to 500 cfs.
Elevation: Put-in 9080 ft., take-out 8300 ft.
Topo Maps: Whitney Reservoir, Christmas Meadows.
Permits: No.
Shuttle Length: About the same as the run.
Access: Highway 150 (Mirror Lake Highway) runs between Kamas and Evanston, WY. This description is of the section between Sulphur Creek Campground (20 miles south of the Utah/Wyoming border) and the East Fork Campground (10 miles south of the border). There are several other access points between these two.

From Sulphur Creek Campground, the river flows gently through meadows and beaver dams. You could skip this slow but beautiful section by putting in around the Beaver View Campground. Below there the current picks up and trees become more of a problem. In some sections the gradient is over 100 ft./mile. There are no major drops, just fast continuous rocky sections. Just above Stillwater Campground, the Stillwater Fork comes in. From this junction on, you are on the Bear River. The increased flow isn't noticeable at first because the gradient eases through there, but the last half mile above the East Fork has more power and bigger waves.

Difficulty: Class 1 to 2.
Length: 4.3 miles.
Average Gradient: 58 ft./mi.
Season: Late May–June.
Time: 1 to 1.5 hours.
Character: Small, narrow, many downed trees.
Levels: 150+ cfs.
Elevation: Put-in 8760 ft., take-out 8500 ft.
Topo Maps: Christmas Meadows.
Permits: No.
Shuttle Length: 4 miles.
Access: Take Highway 150 from Kamas, UT, or Evanston, WY. About
9 miles south of the Utah/Wyoming border is a dirt road going to
Christmas Meadows. Follow this about 3.5 miles to a side road that
crosses the river. Put in at the bridge. The take-out is at the Still-
water Campground just south of the Highway 150 turnoff.

This is a fairly gentle stretch of river that meanders through meadows
and woods to join the Hayden Fork just past the Stillwater Campground
where the two forks become the Bear River. Unfortunately, there are
usually a number of trees that have fallen across the river, so beware.

BEAR RIVER

Difficulty: Class 2 to 3.
Length: 4.5 (16) miles.
Average Gradient: 81 ft./mi.
Season: June.
Time: 1 to 2 hours.
Character: Fast and continuous at first and then breaking into small
channels with high potential for snags.
Levels: 500 to 2000 cfs.
Elevation: Put-in 8300 ft., take-out 7960 ft.
Topo Maps: Deadman Mountain, Myers Reservoir.
Permits: No.

BEAR RIVER - BLACK CANYON

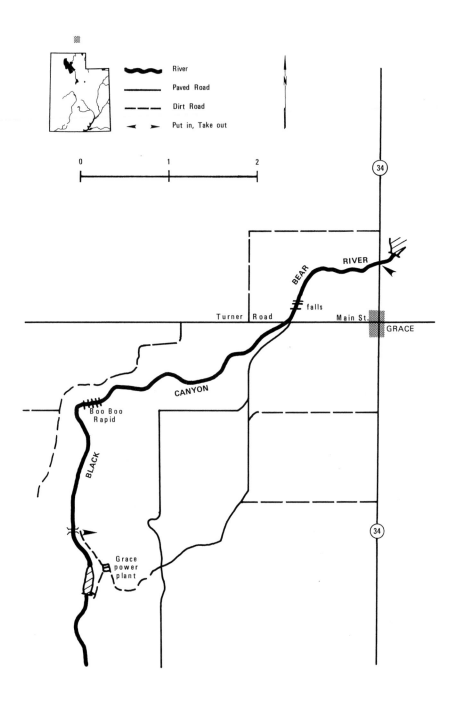

River
Paved Road
Dirt Road
Put in, Take out

0   1   2

34

BEAR RIVER

falls

Turner Road   Main St.
GRACE

CANYON

Boo Boo
Rapid

BLACK

34

Grace
power
plant

Shuttle Length: 4.3 miles.

Access: Take Highway 150 from Kamas, UT, or Evanston, WY. About
2.5 miles south of the Utah/Wyoming border is a potential take-out
at the gauge. I don't know if you are trespassing there. The put-in is
about 7 miles south of the border at the East Fork Campground.

The first couple of miles are splendid boating—fast, continuous, beautiful
scenery. Unfortunately, taking out can be a problem. Most of the land is
private. The first possible take-out that might not involve trespassing is at
the gauge. This involves running some sections where the river breaks up
into small channels that can be completely blocked by trees. You will have
to carry your boats out to the highway. The first place you could get out
at a bridge is at the Chalk Creek Road. This road heads west from Highway 150 about 3.5 miles north of the border at the 90-degree turn in
the highway. This would mean a run of about 16 miles. I have not run
below the gauge. It looks like there are several diversion dams, and there
is a potential for fences across the river.

BLACK CANYON OF THE BEAR

Difficulty: Class 3 to 5-.

Length: 6.8 miles.

Average Gradient: 70 ft./mi.

Season: Dam controlled. 900 cfs is diverted through a pipe to generate
power at the Grace Power Plant. This usually means the river is dry.
Efforts by American Whitewater, Idaho Rivers United, and other
groups and individuals are being made to get scheduled releases.

Time: 3 to 4 hours.

Character: Steep, rocks, holes, falls, basalt gorge.

Levels: >600 cfs.

Elevation: Put-in 5500 feet, take-out 5020 feet.

Topo Maps: Grace, Grace Power Plant.

Permits: No.

Shuttle Length: 7 miles.

Access: From Salt Lake City, it's probably fastest to take I-15 north into
Idaho and take the exit to Soda Springs that goes past Lava Hot
Springs (U.S. 30). Turn south on S.R. 34 and drive to the town of

Grace. The road crosses the Bear River on the north end of town. The put-in is right under the bridge. To get to the take-out, go south into town, go west on Main Street, and go south on the road just before the bridge over the Bear River. (You get a great view of the falls from the bridge.) Follow the road to the Grace Power Plant, through the housing area, and continue upstream to a parking area and the take-out.

Looking across the valley, you would never guess this run existed. The river is hidden 100 feet deep in a basalt gorge. From the put-in, the river and countryside are flat for about a mile. The river then begins cutting into the dark rock, creating a couple of Class 3 rapids and then pooling briefly above a triple falls of Class 4 to 4+ difficulty. You may want to scout your first time through. The first two falls are fairly short, with some maneuvering required. A small pool gives you time to line up for the third drop of 10 to 12 feet that can be run in a variety of places. At flows above 2,000 cfs, there can be a pretty strong reversal at the base.

Many Class 3 and 4 rapids follow the falls with a number of excellent surfing and play spots. The basalt walls become more broken and less sheer. A few hidden holes can catch you by surprise. One rapid you come to spreads wider than the rest. Stay left or you'll end in a boulder field with no route through.

About two-thirds of the way through the run you'll see some houses high up on the bluff ahead. A Class 3 rapid starts below a pool. There's an eddy on the right just above a narrow steep drop. Don't miss this eddy. The drop goes into a river-wide hole and is the beginning of the hardest rapid (Class 5), called Boo Boo. Scout carefully. It's long and rocky and a number of nasty swims have taken place there. Fortunately there is a big pool at the end of the rapid.

The last couple of miles have short, steep, Class 3 to 4 boulder drops. The river then spreads out the last quarter mile with lots of small ledge drops. The take-out is on the left at a large footbridge.

ONEIDA NARROWS OF THE BEAR

Difficulty: Class 1 to 2+.
Length: 6.5 miles from upper bridge to Highway 36 (Mink Creek), another 5 miles to bridge just before Highway 34.

Average Gradient: 18 ft./mi.

Season: Dam controlled, can be run much of summer.

Time: 1 to 6 hours depending on section and play time.

Character: Generally straightforward, along road and farmland with some beautiful narrow sections of canyon, diversion dams, several play spots, easy to scout.

Levels: Can fluctuate rapidly with dam releases, >400 cfs.

Elevation: Put-in 4750 feet, take-out 4560 feet.

Topo Maps: Oneida Narrows Reservoir, Treasureton, Riverdale.

Permits: No.

Shuttle Length: About the same as run.

Access: From Preston, ID, go north on Highway 34. Just after crossing the Bear River, turn right onto Highway 36. A side road goes to the lower take-out at a bridge and picnic area. For the put-in, continue northeast about 3 miles to the signed road for the Oneida Dam. An access spot is available there just below the Highway 34 bridge on river left. Continue up the Oneida Dam road and scout the river as you go, especially the two diversion dams. There are several access points, with the upper one being just below the Oneida Power plant at a bridge.

This is a great beginning to intermediate run. Since a road follows most of the river, you have many options as to what you run. Starting at the bridge below the power plant, you have fairly fast water for about a half-mile and then the river widens and slows for about a mile. The canyon narrows below a picnic area and the river picks up speed, offering rapids and play spots.

The upper diversion dam is usually run on the left but can be run at high water on the right. Portage if you don't like the looks of it. The lower diversion dam is usually run toward the right side. This is just above the Highway 34 access point.

The lower section is a little easier but also has a diversion dam that should be scouted. Portage is easiest on the right.

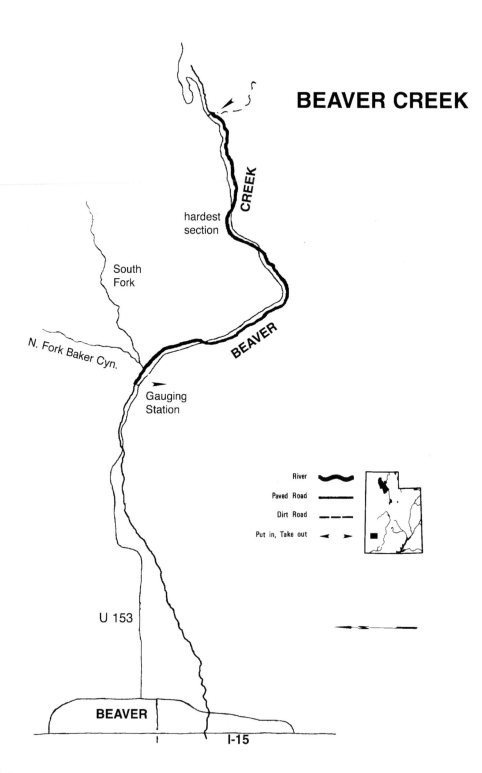

BEAVER CREEK

CREEK

hardest
section

South
Fork

N. Fork Baker Cyn.

BEAVER

Gauging
Station

River	
Paved Road	
Dirt Road	
Put in, Take out	

U 153

BEAVER

I-15

≈ ≈ ≈ BEAVER CREEK

Difficulty: Class 2 to 4+.
Length: 6 miles.
Average Gradient: 150 ft./mi.
Season: May, June.
Time: 2 to 3 hours.
Character: Small, rocky, technical, logs.
Levels: 1.6 to 2.0 on gauge, which is about 4 miles up the canyon.
Elevation: Put-in 7120 ft., take-out 6200 ft.
Topo Maps: Black Ridge, Shelly Baldy Peak.
Permits: No.
Shuttle Length: Same as run.
Access: Highway 153 east of Beaver follows the river, allowing many
access points.

There is a great run from the Kents Lake turnoff (mile marker 10) down
to the gauge. The first 1.5 miles are fairly continuous Class 3. Watch out
for logs. Just after the river goes under the road, it steepens and drops
through a quarter-mile gorge of Class 4+. This should be thoroughly
scouted before running. The gradient eases and the rapids drop back to
Class 3 for another mile or so and then down to Class 2.

JORDAN RIVER
BIG & LITTLE COTTONWOOD CREEKS
AMERICAN FORK RIVER

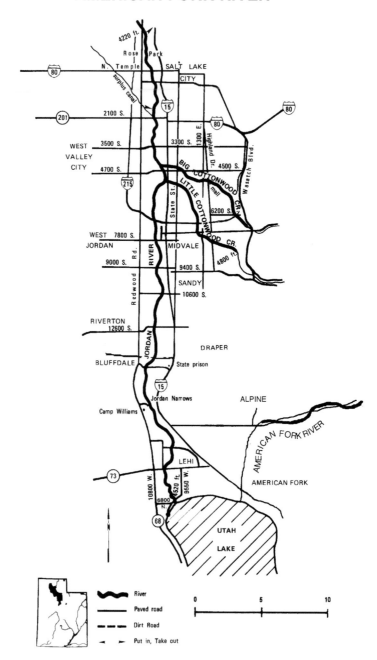

River
Paved road
Dirt Road
Put in, Take out

0   5   10

≈ ≈ ≈ BIG COTTONWOOD CREEK

Difficulty: Class 1 to 4+.
Length: Variable, up to 10 miles in valley.
Average Gradient: 250 ft./mi. canyon, 60 ft./mi. town.
Season: Late May-June.
Time: 1 hour to all day.
Character: Steep, fast, logs, hard to stop in upper. Dams, logs, urban
    hazards in lower.
Levels: 300 to 500 cfs.
Elevation: Mouth of canyon 4960 ft., Jordan River 4235 ft.
Topo Maps: Draper, Sugar House, Salt Lake City South.
Permits: No.
Shuttle Length: Varies but close to length of run,
Access: Highway 152 (Big Cottonwood Canyon), Wasatch Blvd.,
    6200 South, Highland Drive, 4500 South, 3900 South, and many
    other city streets.

Big Cottonwood Creek offers quite a variety of boating, from suicidal to
mellow. Much of the river in the canyon is very steep and rocky with
many trees across, making runs very dangerous.

The best section in the canyon is the bottom couple of miles, from
the Stairs Power plant (Birches picnic area) to the gauge just above the
water treatment plant. I don't know if this is even legal to run, although
I'm sure boating on it has far less effect on the water quality than all the
cars that drive next to the stream. If you run this, walk every inch first to
make sure there aren't any trees across. This is a fast, exciting, pushy
Class 4+ run. Stopping is very difficult if it's running high. A swim could
be ugly and being pinned against a log could be deadly.

The next section is from just below the water treatment plant
(parking area at mouth of canyon) to the catch pond about a mile downstream. The first quarter mile is very fast with several holes to challenge
you. At high flows, this is pushy Class 4+. At low flows, it is rocky Class 4.
It eases a little as you go behind some homes. A low bridge through
there can be an obstacle at high flows, requiring that you tip over to get
under it.

Below the catch pond, the gradient eases somewhat but the river may be more dangerous due to diversion and energy dissipation dams. Many of these are new since the earlier edition of this book. There is very little room to stop above them. Walking around them often means going in someone's back yard. Most are killers to run. One has already claimed the life of a kayaker. Blind turns make it hard to see the dams until you're right on them. Cement walls have replaced most of the rock and wire-mesh walls, making stopping even harder. These walls and dams are in much of the run until after Cottonwood Mall. Be sure to stop at the road just before the Mall, because once you go under it you're committed to a low tunnel and a dangerous drop. Also check the bridges and dam by the parking lot to see if you can make it past them. At high water you won't be able to fit under Highland Drive. Right after is a bridge that may be blocked with a gate.

The river slows below Cottonwood Mall and enters a park where there's a small runnable drop. Then there's a spillway to walk around. Approach 4500 South carefully, as there is a small drop and footbridge before it and sometimes little headroom under it. The river above State Street is channeled between cement walls. Watch out for a pipe across the river blocking the way. The river passes under I-15 in a double tunnel. Big Cottonwood Creek runs into the Jordan River just south of 3900 South.

≈ ≈ ≈ BLACKS FORK

Map: See p. 2.
Difficulty: Class 1 to 2.
Length: 1 to 15 miles.
Average Gradient: 75 ft./mi.
Season: June, early July.
Time: 1 hour to all day.
Character: Mountain stream, small, rocky, logs.
Levels: >300 cfs on either fork, >500 on main. Gauge is a mile below
the confluence of the East and West Forks. Average high is about
1500 cfs.
Elevation: 9000 ft.
Topo Maps: Red Knob, Elizabeth Mountain, Mount Lovenia, Lyman Lake,
Meeks Cabin Reservoir (WY).
Permits: No.
Shuttle Length: About the same as run.
Access: I-80 east to Evanston, WY. Highway 150 south to the East Fork
of the Bear turnoff. Go about 17 miles on this dirt road to the West
Fork Road, about 3 miles farther for the East Fork Road; from there
it's about 6 miles north to the dam at Meeks Cabin Reservoir. You
can also get there from the Mountain View area of Wyoming.

EAST FORK OF BLACKS FORK

A good dirt road takes you to a trailhead just below a ranger station
where a locked gate blocks further vehicle access. The first half mile is
Class 2 and then it eases and winds for 1.5 miles. It then straightens and
steepens with Class 2 rapids again for the rest of the way. Watch out for
logjams. About halfway through the run, on the left, are the remains of
two interesting log cabins.

About a half mile above the confluence with the West Fork, the river
splits into many channels. This continues until about a half mile past the
confluence. Another quarter mile beyond this is a bridge going to the
Hewinta Guard Station, a good place to take out.

Blacks Fork.

WEST FORK OF BLACKS FORK

Shortly after taking the turnoff going up the West Fork, the dirt road splits. Left is a nice access point if you don't have good vehicle clearance. This gives you about 3.5 miles of Class 2 paddling to the bridge going to the East Fork. The river splits up in this stretch for a half mile at a small picnic area. Take out at the East Fork bridge (watch out for a cable there) or continue on down another mile to the bridge going to the Hewinta Guard Station. If you want to go higher up the West Fork to put in, you can drive about 5 miles up the road to where it crosses through the river, giving you an additional 5 miles of easy paddling through open meadow. Going above the river crossing requires four-wheel drive but accesses some beautiful Class 2 to 2+ river.

BLACKS FORK

Put in on the East Fork road where it crosses the West Fork or put in at the bridge going to the Hewinta Guard Station. There is usually a nice surfing wave just below the latter bridge. This is a very enjoyable run. There are usually some play waves and fewer log problems than in the two forks. Watch out for a cable across. It's usually easy to get under. The run takes about a half hour of straight paddling to get to Meeks Cabin Reservoir.

Below Meeks Cabin Reservoir is a great run. It's about a 10-minute walk down a dirt road to put in below the dam. If you have four-wheel drive you may be able to drive this. The river is fast and continuous Class 1 and 2 all the way. There is some splitting of channels, but it's not bad. Before long you go under a bridge. In another mile or so, you go under an old log bridge. One of the best rapids is right after this. A third bridge is at a fisherman access spot. There is a good take-out on the left, just below the bridge. The river splits a little more after this, with increased logjam potential. In about 1.5 miles there is another fisherman access point. It is hard to see and you could totally miss it by taking a right channel above it. So if you are going this far, be sure you can recognize the spot. If you miss this, there isn't a good take-out for quite a while and you will be dealing with potential problems of major channel splitting, logs, fences, and diversion dams.

≈ ≈ ≈ BLACKSMITH FORK

Difficulty: Class 1 to 4.
Length: 1 to 10 miles.
Average Gradient: 80 ft./mi. lower section.
Season: May, June.
Time: 1 to 5 hours.
Character: Small, rocky, logs, dams, low bridges, brushy.
Levels: Normal high is about 500 cfs, run at 250 to 500 cfs.
Elevation: Hyrum City Park 5180 ft., mouth of canyon 4800 ft.
Topo Maps: Hardware Ranch, Logan Peak, Porcupine Reservoir, Paradise, Logan.
Permits: No.
Shuttle Length: About the same as river run.
Access: From U.S. 89 near Logan, take Highway 101 or 165 to Hyrum
and then Highway 101 up Blacksmith Fork Canyon. The road follows
the river in the canyon.

This river isn't run often—maybe because it isn't often runnable. When
the snowpack is high, there is great potential there. Most of the year it's
nice wading and fishing. Much of the land along it is private, so pick your
access points carefully.

The river above the dam (about milepost 15) is generally mellow
and meandering and bushy with a few faster rocky stretches, especially in
the upper parts. Watch out for low bridges, fences, and moose. Below the
dam, the half mile down to Hyrum City Park is very brushy and steep.
There is a low bridge with a hole above it at higher water right above
the park. The river flattens more down to the Shenoah picnic site, then
becomes faster to just above the Left Hand Fork (about milepost 13),
then eases greatly as it goes through private property. There are several
low bridges that you probably won't fit under.

The most exciting stretch starts just below milepost 11. About mile
10.5, you pass the remains of a dam. There is still a drop of a couple feet.
Check this out before running it, as it can be hard to stop right above it.
For the rest of the run, especially at high water, you will need Class 4
skills to handle the fast, steep, tight turns and avoid the logs that often
block the way. Lower water is a little easier. You will go under the road
twice. The bottom mile of the canyon seems to have a lot of logs across.

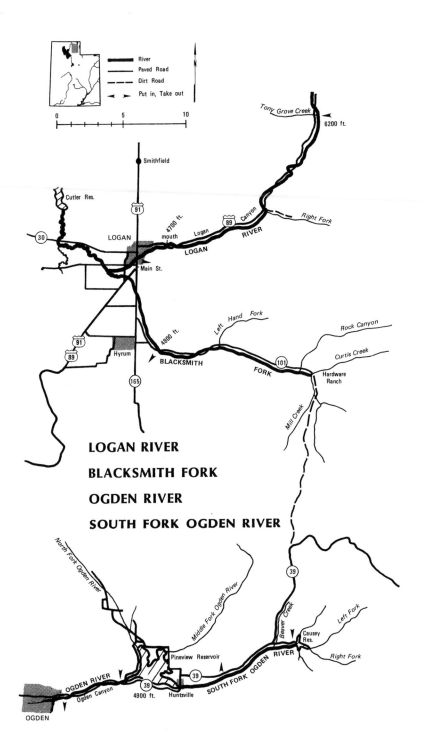

LOGAN RIVER

BLACKSMITH FORK

OGDEN RIVER

SOUTH FORK OGDEN RIVER

≈ ≈ ≈ BRUNEAU and JARBIDGE RIVERS

Difficulty: Class 3 to 5- (P).
Length: Jarbidge 29.5 miles, Bruneau 39 miles.
Average Gradient: Jarbidge 45 ft./mi., Bruneau 30 ft./mi.
Season: Late April into June.
Time: 2 to 5 days.
Character: Deep basalt gorges, boulder drops, occasional logs, remote, raftable.
Levels: Best at 900 to 2000 cfs.
Elevation: Put-in 4980 ft., take-out 2600 ft.
Topo Maps: Dishpan, Poison Butte, The Arch, Inside Lakes, Indian Hot Springs, Stiff Tree Draw, Winter Camp, Austin Butte, Crowbar Gulch, Hot Spring, Sugar Valley.
Permits: Yes, but no fee or limit. BLM, (208) 384-3300.
Shuttle Length: 74 miles of mostly dirt road. Contact the Jumbo's Auto Service in Bruneau for shuttle help, (208) 845-2150.
Access: To get to the take-out, turn off I-84 on Highway 78 and then 51 to get to the town of Bruneau. If you have any questions, stop at the Sinclair station. You can't miss it. Take the road heading southeast out of town. In about 8 miles you will come to the Blackstone-Grasmere Road. Turn right and cross the river. The take-out is in about 2 miles. Stay left at junctions (follow the signs). For the put-in, go back to the Blackstone-Grasmere Road and turn right on the Clover–Three Creek Road. Follow this dirt road for about 60 miles. (About halfway through this stretch, about a mile south of where you cross the East Fork of the Bruneau, is the turnoff if you are going to run only the Bruneau. You will need four-wheel drive.) Turn right on Jarbidge Road and go 9 miles to Murphy Hot Springs. Drive 2 miles downstream along the East Fork of the Jarbidge to where it joins the West Fork and put in. There is camping there.

These two rivers have cut incredible basalt gorges in a remote area of southern Idaho. River runners are asked to obtain permits from the BLM. The BLM will also send you information about the run if requested.

There are many small rapids and several major ones. The big ones are all boulder piles and should be scouted. The first hard rapid, Sevy

BRUNEAU & JARBIDGE RIVERS

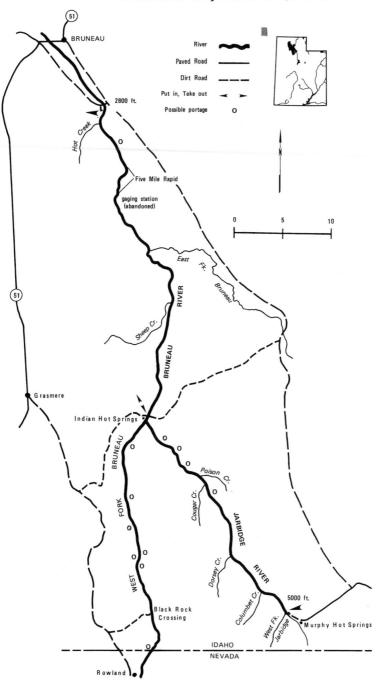

River	
Paved Road	
Dirt Road	
Put in, Take out	
Possible portage	O

≈ 21

Jarbidge River.

Bruneau River.

Falls, is about 16 miles from the put-in. The next 1.5 miles have lots of good rapids. Four miles farther is the second of the harder rapids, Wally's Wallow. The hardest, Jarbidge Falls, is another 5 miles down. Where you run these varies from year to year, depending on where logs have caught. Rafts may have to be portaged even when the slots are free of trees because they are so narrow.

Jarbidge Falls is fairly obvious if you watch for a large rockslide on the right. As you approach it, you will see a huge boulder that looks like it blocks the whole river. Do not go beyond it without scouting. You may want to get out well above it. There is a portage trail on the left. Watch out for poison ivy. The rapid is a long, tight, steep, boulder-choked rapid of Class 4+ to 5 difficulty. The top part is the hardest. Kayakers (or C-1) who don't want to run the top can put in partway through and avoid some of the portage.

In about 3 miles, the Jarbidge River joins the West Fork of the Bruneau to form the Bruneau River. About a mile later you come to Indian Hot Springs on the left. A new larger tub has made it more enjoyable. Steep rough roads come in there from either side. The one on the right (east) is the most common access for those who want to run just the Bruneau.

Shortly below the hot spring you enter Bruneau Canyon. The first rapid (Cave Rapid) goes right into an undercut cliff and makes an almost 180-degree turn. A couple miles of easy water allow time to soak in the incredible view. Rapids are scattered along the next 11 miles. Sheep Creek enters on the left and offers good hiking. The rapids become a little more challenging as you approach the East Fork of the Bruneau, which comes in on the right about 9 miles past Sheep Creek. The canyon walls become less sheer.

Five-Mile Rapid starts about 8 miles below the East Fork. At low flows the rapid is really a series of rapids with short breaks between. At high flows the drops blend together for most of the first 3 miles, with many rapids in the next 2 miles. This is delightful Class 3 to 4.

A few miles after Five-Mile Rapid, you will come to a rapid that splits around an island. Scout on the left if you're not sure where to run it. The BLM take-out is 3 miles farther. If you continue beyond there, you will run into two diversion dams. These can be run at certain water levels, but it's not recommended. You also run into private land where access is a problem.

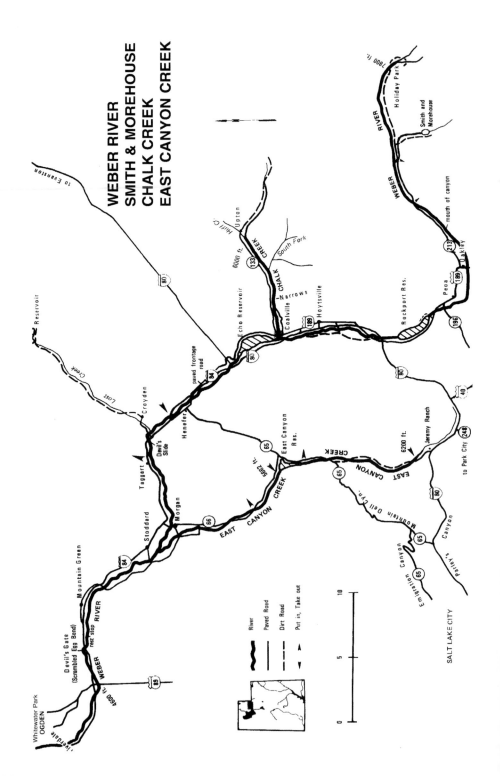

WEBER RIVER
SMITH & MOREHOUSE
CHALK CREEK
EAST CANYON CREEK

River
Paved Road
Dirt Road
Put in, Take out

≈ ≈ ≈ CHALK CREEK

Difficulty: Class 1 to 2.
Length: 1 to 15 miles.
Average Gradient: 40 ft./mi. in steepest section.
Season: May, June.
Time: One-half hour to 4 hours.
Character: Open mountain farmland with fairly smooth water except for the Narrows, which is swift and brushy.
Levels: >200 cfs.
Elevation: Put-in 5800 ft. or higher, take-out 5740 ft.
Topo Maps: Coalville, Turner Hollow, Upton.
Shuttle Length: About the same as run.
Permits: No.
Access: From I-80 take the Coalville exit and go east on U-133. This mostly follows the river.

Chalk Creek would be a pleasant run except that fences block it and it's surrounded by private property. The landowners probably won't be happy to see you and may try to chase you away.

The best part to run is the Narrows, about 2.5 miles above Coalville. The river cuts through a small gorge and hides the road for about a half mile. The scenery is pleasant but the brushy banks make stopping difficult through this Class 2 stretch. A bridge just below the Narrows is a good take-out.

COAL CREEK

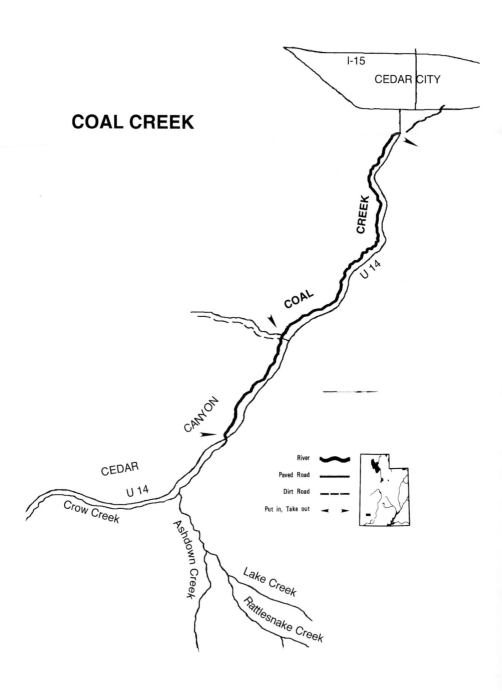

I-15

CEDAR CITY

CREEK

U 14

COAL

CANYON

CEDAR

U 14

Crow Creek

Ashdown Creek

Lake Creek

Rattlesnake Creek

River
Paved Road
Dirt Road
Put in, Take out

≈ ≈ ≈ COAL CREEK

Difficulty: Class 3 to 4 (P).

Length: 5 to 7 miles.

Average Gradient: 130 ft./mi.

Season: Late April, early May.

Time: 1 to 3 hours.

Character: Steep, fast, continuous, several large man-made falls to portage.

Levels: >250 cfs.

Elevation: Put-in 6500 ft., take-out 5860 ft.

Topo Maps: Cedar City, Flanigan Arch.

Permits: No.

Shuttle Length: Same as run.

Access: Coal Creek runs through Cedar City. Put in anywhere along Highway 14 heading toward Cedar Breaks. A good put-in is about 5 miles up the canyon from the side road to Kolob Reservoir. There is a good place to take out at the park on the east edge of Cedar

Coal Creek portage.

City, just above where the river goes under the highway. Water and a bathroom can be found there.

This is a different kind of river in that it is mostly Class 3 with Class 6 consequences. It is fast and continuous with some logjam potential but with a wide enough channel that you can usually see things in time to stop. The danger is the huge man-made falls that offer little warning with little slowing in speed above them. It would be easy to blunder off one. The more than 20-foot drops (onto rocks and cement) would be disastrous, not to mention the hydraulics in the smaller cascading drops after. From the Kolob turnoff to the park is about 5 miles with 3 major falls and a much smaller runnable (scout first) drop at a gauge just above the last falls.

You could put in above the Kolob Reservoir road at several possible points and add up to 2 more miles of slightly steeper paddling. At that point, the highway climbs away from the river near a huge set of drops.

Belknap's waterproof "Canyonlands River Guide" is an excellent mile-by-mile map for the following sections of the Colorado River.

HORSETHIEF AND RUBY CANYONS

Difficulty: Mainly Class 1, a little Class 2.
Length: 27 miles.
Average Gradient: 5 ft./mi.
Season: All year; can freeze in winter.
Time: 1 to 2 days.
Character: Mostly flat, open, desert river in some beautiful canyons.
Levels: Any, ranges from 1000 to over 50,000 cfs.
Elevation: Put-in 4420 ft., take-out 4300 ft.
Topo Maps: Mack, Ruby Canyon, Bitter Creek Well, Westwater.
Permits: No.
Shuttle Length: 40 miles.
Access: To get to the put-in, take the Loma exit from I-70, turn south, and immediately turn left on a dirt road. Follow it down to the river. To get to the take-out, turn off I-70 at the Westwater exit and follow the road to the Westwater ranger station.

This beginner's run, besides offering pleasant paddling, also offers great hiking. Horsethief Canyon begins about a mile downstream from the Loma put-in. The sandstone walls rise around you fairly quickly. Rattlesnake Canyon, on the left, offers excellent hiking with views of some arches. There are several small riffles below there. After the canyon widens out, Salt Creek comes in at about mile 10, bringing with it the railroad, which accompanies you to the Westwater take-out.

The canyon walls begin to close in again and you enter Ruby Canyon. At about mile 14, just before Mee Canyon, some interesting balanced rocks and hollowed-out cliffs appear on the left. You arrive at Black Rocks Rapid at about mile 17. The higher the water the more turbulence you get there. Beginning canoeists may find this a bit challenging at higher water levels. The area gets its name from the ancient black Precambrian rock that lies exposed. Just below this area, on the left, is one of the

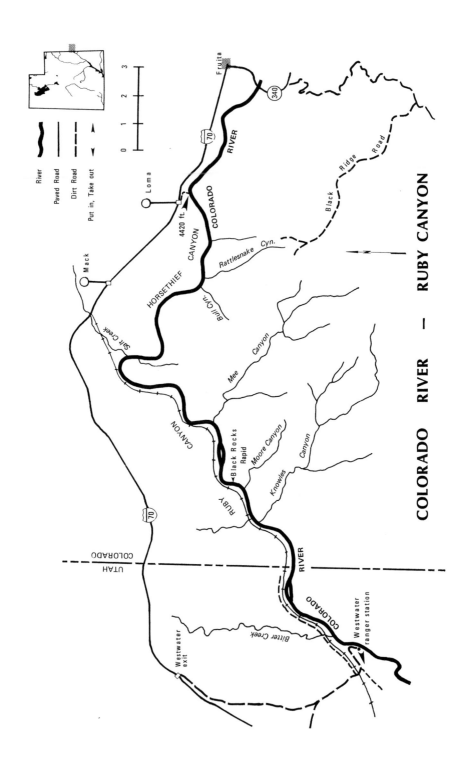

COLORADO RIVER — RUBY CANYON

most popular campsites. This is by Moore Canyon. Knowles Canyon is not too much farther. These canyons offer excellent hikes.

The last 4 or 5 miles are more open with some ranching going on. Check with the BLM on what is private land and what is public. Be sure to get out at the Westwater Ranger Station unless you have a permit and are ready for the Class 3 to 4 whitewater.

WESTWATER CANYON

Difficulty: Mainly Class 3, a little Class 4.
Length: 17 miles.
Average Gradient: 9 ft./mi.
Season: All year; can freeze in winter.
Time: 1 to 2 days.
Character: Pool-drop, narrow desert canyon.
Levels: All, ranges from 1000 to over 50,000 cfs.
Elevation: Put-in 4300 ft., take-out 4145 ft.
Topo Maps: Westwater, Agate, Big Triangle.
Permits: Yes: BLM, Westwater Permit Office, (435) 259-7012, http://www.blm.gov/ut/st/en/fo/moab/recreation/river_recreation/westwater_canyon.html.
Shuttle Length: 32 miles.
Access: Take the Westwater exit from I-70 and follow the road to the ranger station. Bathrooms and camping are available there. You can also take the ranch exit to the west and follow the north frontage road east to a dirt road that goes under the freeway along Westwater Wash and connects with the paved road from the Westwater exit. This can be slick if really wet. The take-out is by Cisco. Depending on which direction you're coming from, take one of the two Cisco exits off I-70 and follow several miles to Cisco (very few inhabitants and no food or gas). At Cisco take the road going southeast behind the town. In almost 3 miles the road splits; take the left fork to the river. There are toilets and parking.

Westwater is the place to test your ability to handle the bigger sections of the Colorado River such as Cataract Canyon. The rapids aren't as big but they can be just as pushy. The river is funneled into a much narrower canyon than almost anywhere else on the Colorado. This creates

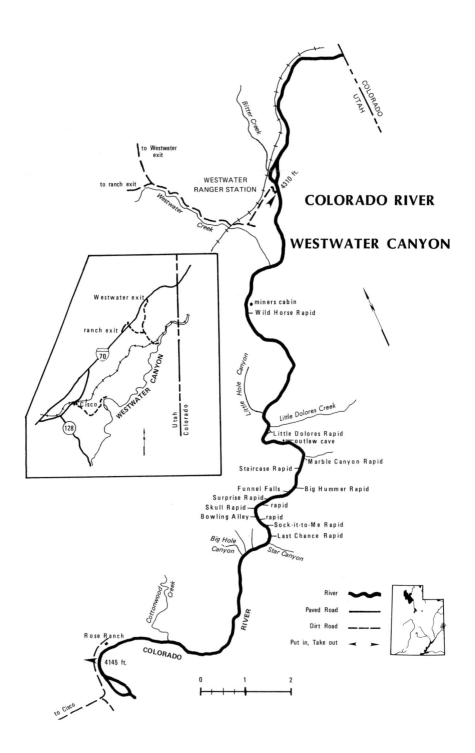

COLORADO RIVER

WESTWATER CANYON

miners cabin
Wild Horse Rapid

Little Hole Canyon

Little Dolores Creek

Little Dolores Rapid
outlaw cave

Marble Canyon Rapid

Staircase Rapid

Funnel Falls — Big Hummer Rapid
Surprise Rapid
Skull Rapid — rapid
Bowling Alley — rapid
Sock-it-to-Me Rapid
Last Chance Rapid

Big Hole
Canyon

Star Canyon

Cottonwood Creek

Rose Ranch
4145 ft.
COLORADO

to Cisco

RIVER

River	
Paved Road	
Dirt Road	
Put in, Take out	◄ ►

to Westwater exit

WESTWATER
RANGER STATION

to ranch exit

Westwater Creek

4310 ft.

Bitter Creek

COLORADO
UTAH

Westwater exit

ranch exit

70

Cisco

WESTWATER CANYON

Utah
Colorado

128

0   1   2

tremendous power and interesting turbulence, especially at high water. High-water hydraulics can be challenging for smaller craft. A swim at high flows could last for several miles. Low water can be challenging for large rafts trying to fit through narrow slots. Flows below 2000 cfs are especially tight. Camping spots are limited; however, the run can easily be done in a day.

The first 3 miles are fairly gentle and the canyon more open. Just before the massive cliffs on the right, the river splits into several channels. As they come together, the first rapids start. An old dugout cabin on the left is a popular stopping point just below the first rapid. The next 4 miles have numerous Class 1 and 2 rapids with many play spots for kayakers and canoeists. The rapids pick up after a big bend to the right, just above where Little Dolores Creek comes in. A short hike up Little Dolores Creek takes you to a seasonal pool and waterfall. The lower of the two Little Dolores Rapids is the most popular play spot of the trip at flows of up to about 7000 cfs. A wave hole offers a chance to cartwheel, surf, and pop up until you're almost too tired to paddle out. Shortly below this, on the left, is the "outlaw cave."

The heart of the canyon starts where Marble Canyon comes in. The rapids come in fairly quick succession for 2.5 miles and are Class 3 to 4- in difficulty. The higher the flow the more they start to blend together. At 30,000 cfs and up, you basically have one long rapid. At most flows, Marble Canyon Rapid is the longest. It is followed by Staircase, with nice surfing on large standing waves. After a short break and a couple of small drops, Big Hummer Rapid appears on a right turn where a large rock blocks the left center at lower flows. Another short flat section leads to a rock sticking up on the left and a horizon line marking Funnel Falls. At the bottom of this drop, waves pound you from both sides and tend to push you to the wall on the right. Two short drops, Surprise and an unnamed one, keep the excitement up between Funnel Falls and Skull Rapid.

Skull Rapid is usually the toughest rapid. Rock fall on the left has narrowed the river to where it backs up, then accelerates rapidly through the narrow opening and crashes over the huge boulders hidden under water. There is a small landing spot on the top left at low to medium flows where you can get out and scout. The bottom of the rapid is an almost river-wide wave hole at flows between 3000 and 15,000 cfs. Below this level, the huge rock creating the hole sticks out. Other rocks also stick above the surface, creating a challenging slalom course. Above

The Bowling Alley, Westwater Canyon of the Colorado River.

this level, it starts to wash out. Immediately following the hole, the river slams into the cliff with most of it going left. The rest of the water goes into the Room of Doom on the right, where a powerful eddy tends to trap everything. Boats have floated into the wall and flipped or been pinned, with at least one death resulting. Boats that avoid the wall but wash into the Room of Doom can have a very difficult time getting out. You may need to throw a rope across the river and be pulled out. Some have resorted to hauling their rafts up the cliff and carrying them downstream until they find a place to lower back into the river.

Bowling Alley is the next major rapid. At flows below 4500 cfs, the steep waves, with eddies on either side, create an ideal place to play. Next comes a small unnamed rapid and then Sock-It-to-Me, where a steep drop accelerates you into curling, converging side waves that do what the name says. For those who like getting pounded, it can be a great play spot. A swim there, often means getting sucked into the "magnetic wall" on the left, where it can be tricky to get out.

The last major rapid, Last Chance, has a large boulder blocking the center of the river except at flows above about 7000 cfs, when a huge wave is formed. Low flows create steep curling waves on the left. Two small rapids follow with play spots at certain lower flow levels. Six miles of flat but scenic water bring you to the Cisco take-out below Rose Ranch. Bathrooms, boat ramp, and parking are available.

CISCO TO HITTLE BOTTOM

Difficulty: Class 1.
Length: Up to 24 miles.
Average Gradient: 4 ft./mi.
Season: All year; can freeze.
Time: 2 days.
Character: Flat water, open desert canyon.
Levels: All.
Elevation: Put-in 4145 ft., take-out 4100 ft.
Topo Maps: Big Triangle, Cisco, Dewey.
Permits: No.
Shuttle Length: 26 miles.
Access: The put-in is by Cisco. Depending on which direction you're coming from, take one of the two Cisco exits off I-70 and follow several miles to Cisco (very few inhabitants and no food or gas). At Cisco take the road going southeast behind the town. In almost 3 miles the road splits; left goes to the higher put-in, right goes to Fish Ford. To get to the take-out go west from Cisco and turn south on U-128. The take-out is at the boat ramp and campground at Hittle Bottom off U-128. There are several other access points mentioned in the text below.

The Colorado River flows fairly smoothly through a more open canyon in this section. This is probably the best stretch to get away from the crowds. In the 4 miles from the Cisco landing to Fish Ford, the river winds around several islands. Road access is available at this point. Another 5 or 6 miles take you to some ranches and Hotel Bottom. U-128 comes in just below there and then the Dolores River comes in on the left. In about 1.5 miles, you go under the old and then the new Dewey Bridges. There is river access just below there on the left.

The canyon walls soon rise and narrow, forming a short canyon of Wingate Sandstone for 6 miles below Dewey. Partway through, on the

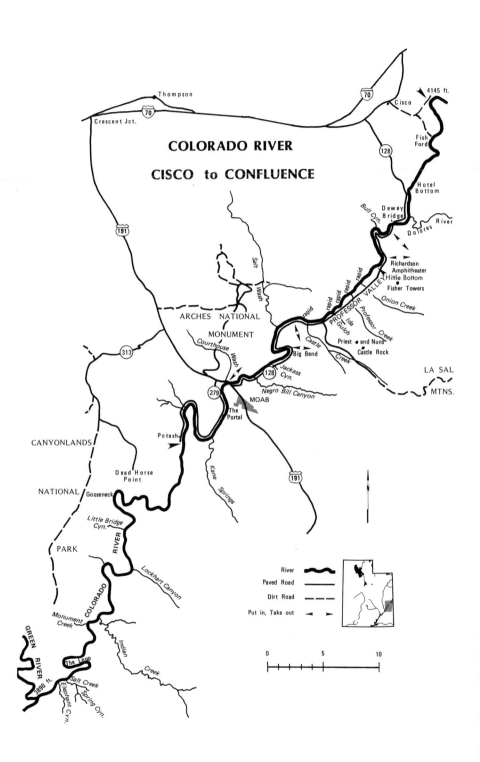

COLORADO RIVER

CISCO to CONFLUENCE

Thompson

Crescent Jct.

70

Cisco

4145 ft.

Fish Ford

128

Hotel Bottom

191

Bull Cyn.

Dewey Bridge

Dolores River

rapid

rapid

rapid

rapid

Richardson Amphitheater

Hittle Bottom

Fisher Towers

Onion Creek

PROFESSOR VALLEY

Professor Creek

Ida Gulch

Salt Wash

ARCHES NATIONAL

MONUMENT

Courthouse Wash

313

Castle Creek

Priest and Nuns

Castle Rock

LA SAL MTNS.

rapid

Big Bend

Castle

128

Jackass Cyn.

279

Negro Bill Canyon

MOAB

The Portal

CANYONLANDS

Potash

Dead Horse Point

NATIONAL

Gooseneck

Kane Springs

191

PARK

Little Bridge Cyn.

COLORADO RIVER

Lockhart Canyon

Monument Creek

GREEN RIVER

3880 ft.

The Loop

Salt Creek

Elephant Cyn.

Spring Cyn.

Indian Creek

River
Paved Road
Dirt Road
Put in, Take out

0   5   10

36 ≈

right, is a nice short hike up Bull Canyon. As you go around the sharp corner below this, one of the most spectacular river scenes comes into view, especially in early spring. The river fills the bottom, with the Fisher Towers behind, all backed by the snow-capped La Sal Mountains. Below this is Hittle Bottom with its boat ramp, bathrooms, and campground.

HITTLE BOTTOM TO MOAB

Difficulty: Class 1 to 3.
Length: Up to 24 miles.
Average Gradient: 5 ft./mi.
Season: All year; can freeze.
Time: 1 to 2 days.
Character: Spectacular desert scenery, flat water interspersed with rapids created by flash floods from side canyons.
Levels: All.
Elevation: Put-in 4100 ft., take-out 3965 ft.
Topo Maps: Dewey, Fisher Towers, Big Bend, The Windows Section, Moab.
Permits: No.
Shuttle Length: Roughly the same as river length.
Access: U-128 follows the river. Get there from I-70 and the Moab or Cisco exits depending on the direction from which you are coming.

Below Hittle Bottom, the river peacefully enters Professor Valley. Castleton Tower and the Priest and Nuns are prominent formations ahead and left. Much of the land is private, so access points are limited. In 2 miles you come to Onion Creek Rapid, created by the boulders brought in by the flash flooding of the creek. Sandy beaches below on the right are perfect for a lunch spot. A little farther, at lower flows, the smaller channel to the right, around an island, offers fun playing for kayaks. A mile below is Professor Creek Rapid. The next major rapid, marked by a large cliff on the left, is Cloudburst or "New" rapid. It was formed by a flash flood during a thunderstorm in 1976. At lower flows, two rocks jut out in the middle with a runnable tongue between, offering play potential for kayaks. At high flows, large standing waves form with a large whirlpool on the left. At really high flows, an almost river-wide giant wave forms where many kayaks at a time can surf for hours.

In another mile, on a sharp right bend, is Ida Gulch Rapid. In the lower part of the rapid, the river splits. At high flows, the right side pushes somewhat against the right wall, where a couple of violent eddies form. The left split passes a good access point with a parking area and bathrooms. Where the two channels come together, the turbulence creates a good kayak play spot.

Fast current and small riffles mark the next mile. The river then slows down, the calm before the storm, as the water backs up behind White's (Castle Creek) Rapid. This is the big rapid of the area. The river bends right, hits the wall, and bends left to start the rapid. You tend to be pushed to the outside of the bend (right), which is also where the holes and rocks are. The best run is following the biggest waves down the center. The safest is left of center. The fast water continues for another half mile. About a mile below there is another access point with a big parking area, a large beach, and a bathroom.

Several rapids break up the flat water in the section from there to the main take-out below Salt Wash. In another 2 miles, Big Bend offers camping, river access, and a couple of rapids. The last 6 miles above the Moab bridge are flat and slow but very scenic, passing Negro Bill Canyon with its wonderful hiking and, shortly after, Updraft Arch on the left. There are places you can get out on either side of the river, just above the bridge.

There are many places to camp along the river corridor. Be sure you have read the rules posted along the road. Camping is allowed only in designated sites, with some of them requiring that you have your own toilet. Please do all you can to minimize your impact, as this is a heavily used area.

MOAB TO POTASH

The Colorado River curves through the open Moab Valley past the Matheson Preserve and cuts into a narrow canyon at The Portal. Beautiful scenery and flat water are in store for those who float this 16-mile stretch. No permits are required. This is a nice day run in a canoe or touring kayak. U-279 follows the river.

POTASH TO LAKE POWELL (Cataract Canyon)

Difficulty: Class 1 to 4.
Length: 49 miles to confluence with the Green River, 65 miles to Lake

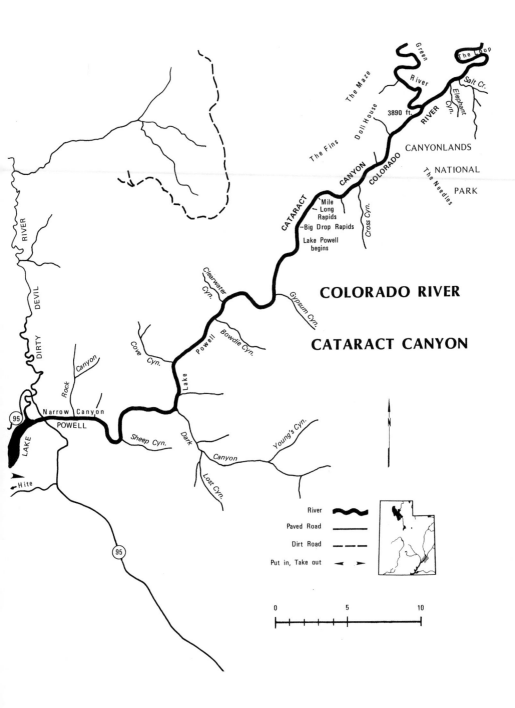

The Loop

Green River

Salt Cr.

The Maze

Elephant Cyn.

Doll House

3890 ft.

COLORADO RIVER

The Fins

CATARACT CANYON

CANYONLANDS

NATIONAL

The Needles

PARK

Cross Cyn.

Mile Long Rapids

Big Drop Rapids

Lake Powell begins

Clearwater Cyn.

Gypsum Cyn.

COLORADO RIVER

CATARACT CANYON

Cove Cyn.

Bowdie Cyn.

Lake Powell

RIVER

DIRTY DEVIL

Rock Canyon

Narrow Canyon

95

POWELL

LAKE

Sheep Cyn.

Dark

Young's Cyn.

Canyon

Lost Cyn.

Hite

95

River

Paved Road

Dirt Road

Put in, Take out

N

0   5   10

≈ 39

Triple Rig in Big Drop 2 in Cataract Canyon of the Colorado River.

Powell, 98 miles to Hite.

Average Gradient: 1 ft./mi. above Green River, 16 ft./mi. in Cataract.

Season: All year; can freeze.

Time: 4 or more days.

Character: Scenic desert canyons, mostly flatwater with all the white-water in about a 12-mile section of pool-drop type rapids. At high flows, the rapids start blending together and the waves are huge.

Levels: All.

Elevation: Put-in 3925 ft., take-out 3700 ft.

Topo Maps: Moab, Gold Bar Canyon, Shafer Basin, Musselman Arch, Lockhart Basin, Monument Basin, The Loop, Spanish Bottom, Cross Canyon, Teapot Rock, Bowdie Canyon East, Bowdie Canyon West, Sewing Machine, Copper Point, Hite North.

Permits: Yes: NPS, Canyonlands National Park, (435) 259-4351, http://www.nps.gov/cany/planyourvisit/rivers.htm.

Shuttle Length: 165 miles.

Access: To get to the put-in from I-70, go south on U.S. 191 toward

Moab, turn west on U-279 to the launching area just past Potash. To get to the take-out from I-70, take the Hanksville exit and follow U-24 to Hanksville, then go south on U-95 to Lake Powell. Cross the bridges over the Dirty Devil and the Colorado River and turn west to Hite Marina.

This stretch offers many side canyons to hike, some with ruins and petroglyphs. It is interesting to drive to Dead Horse Point before your trip and see the view from up high. About 10 miles below Potash you'll get a close-up view of what you looked down on from Dead Horse Point. At The Loop, the river doubles back on itself twice, covering about 6 miles in a straight-line distance of 1 mile. It's fun to hike over the first saddle and be picked up by a boat on the other side. The saddle at the second loop doesn't offer the same opportunity—unless you are willing to do a little cliff jumping into water of unknown depth. About 1.5 miles above the confluence, the river is pinched in at The Slide. At some levels this creates a few riffles.

Three miles below the confluence is a large open area on the right called Spanish Bottom. There is a great hike there up to the Doll House. Cataract Canyon starts just below. The rapids are frequent and exciting for the next 12 miles. At low flows, under 10,000 cfs, the rapids are rocky Class 2 to 3+ with calm sections between rapids. At high flows, the rapids are Class 3 to 4+, with huge waves, violent holes, and many of the calm sections gone. Rapid 7 develops monstrous but forgiving waves. Mile Long becomes one long rapid and Big Drops 1, 2, and 3 have very little break between them. The Big Drops at high flows have flipped so many rafts that the Park Service usually has a powerboat stationed below them to do rescues until the flows drop below 50,000 cfs.

When Lake Powell is full it backs up to about a half mile below the Big Drops. Most people arrange for some means of motoring out the 33 miles to Hite Marina, since the river's current is swallowed up in the reservoir and you often have strong upstream winds to fight. There are a number of possible side hikes to do in the Lake Powell section, but good campsites can be harder to find.

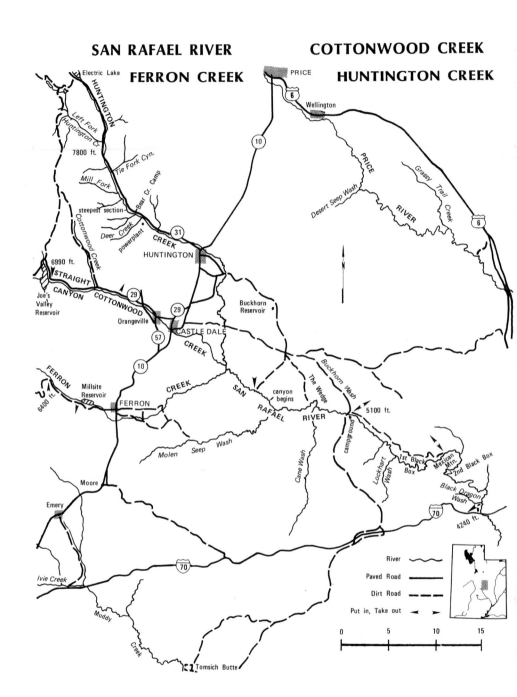

SAN RAFAEL RIVER
FERRON CREEK

COTTONWOOD CREEK
HUNTINGTON CREEK

Electric Lake

HUNTINGTON

Left Fork
Huntington Cr.

7800 ft.

Tie Fork Cyn.

Mill Fork

Bear Cr. Camp

steepest section

Cottonwood Creek

Deer Creek

powerplant

CREEK

HUNTINGTON

6990 ft.

STRAIGHT

Joe's
Valley
Reservoir

CANYON

COTTONWOOD

29

29

Orangeville

57

CASTLE DALE

CREEK

10

FERRON

6400 ft.

Millsite
Reservoir

FERRON

CREEK

SAN

RAFAEL

RIVER

Molen

Seep

Wash

Moore

Emery

Ivie Creek

70

Muddy

Creek

Tomsich Butte

PRICE

6

Wellington

10

PRICE

RIVER

Grassy Trail Creek

6

Desert Seep Wash

N

Buckhorn
Reservoir

Buckhorn Wash

The Wedge

canyon
begins

5100 ft.

campground

Cane Wash

Lockhart Wash

1st Black
Box

Mexican Mtn.

2nd Black Box

Black Dragon
Wash

70

4240 ft.

River

Paved Road

Dirt Road

Put in, Take out

0   5   10   15

≈ ≈ ≈ **COTTONWOOD CREEK**
(Straight Canyon)

Difficulty: Class 3 to 4.
Length: 8 miles.
Average Gradient: 90 ft./mi.
Season: June (dam controlled).
Time: 2 to 4 hours.
Character: Large boulders, logs, tight turns, narrow twisting drops.
Levels: >250 cfs.
Elevation: Put-in 6800 ft., take-out 6080 ft.
Topo Maps: Joe's Valley Reservoir, Mahogany Point, Red Point.
Permits: No.
Shuttle Length: Same as river length.
Access: From Price, drive south on U-10 to just before Castle Dale, take
U-29 to the river.

During the high-water years of the early 1980s, we worked our way
south from Price looking for new rivers to run. When we drove up the
road to Joes Valley Reservoir, we couldn't believe our eyes. We thought
we'd died and gone to heaven or at least made a wrong turn and ended
up in Idaho. Here was a river we'd never heard of anyone running with
almost continuous Class 3 to 4 whitewater, large boulders creating lots
of eddies and play spots, with translucent turquoise water instead of the
usual brown. This is probably my favorite run in the state. Unfortunately,
the river doesn't always have boatable flows. We happened to have over
1000 cfs on our first run. That's still to me the finest level, but it's quite
rare. Fortunately, it can be run down to about 250 cfs. Low flows are easier and less pushy. The best play level may be 450 to 700. This area has
also become popular for bouldering, so you may be able to get in some
of that as well.

It used to be easy to walk down the face of the dam to put in. This has
been blocked and signed to keep out. There is a lower road going up to the
dam that we have used but it is usually gated, so you have to walk and
carry your boat. Just downstream from this road is a tree across the river.
Since you usually have to get out to go around the tree, this may be the
best place to put in. You do miss some fine whitewater by starting this low.

Cottonwood Creek.

Much of the run can be road scouted and it's a good idea to do this. Mostly, though, you can eddy scout the river. If you can't see whether a chute is clear, get out and scout, as logs get caught in hidden places, creating some serious pin potential.

The best paddling is not really on Cottonwood Creek but is actually in Straight Canyon. The gradient eases and the canyon opens about where the actual Cottonwood Creek enters. The river then goes away from the road for about a mile where it is Class 1 and 2. The river swings back to the road and you enter a small gorge with faster current and Class 2 to 3 rapids, with the last rapid being the rockiest. There is a good take-out at a bridge shortly after (just past mile marker 13). Below there the river flattens and swings away from the road over against a cliff where a diversion dam blocks the way. Watch out for barbed-wire fences if you go below this.

There is limited camping along the river and a large campground on the far side of Joes Valley Reservoir.

LOWRY WATER

In late May or early June, this stream running into the north end of Joes Valley Reservoir can sometimes be run. Put in by the Reeder Subdivision and take out on the lake. This gives you about 1.5 miles of Class 1 and 2. Watch out for logs.

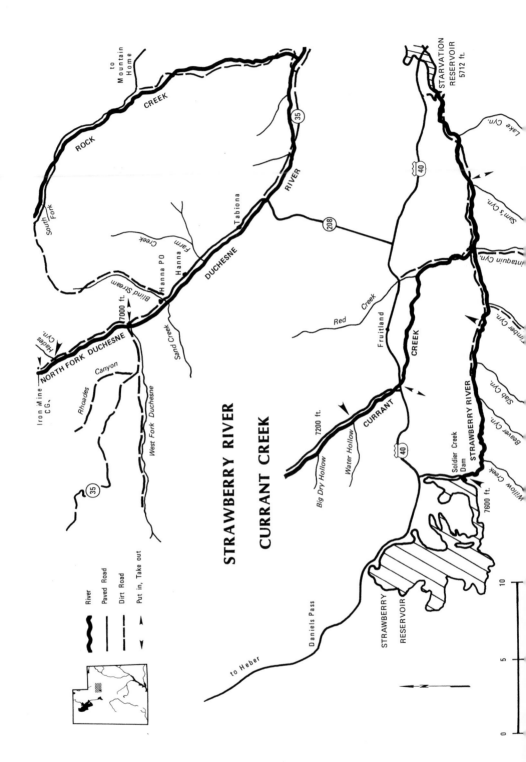

STRAWBERRY RIVER

CURRANT CREEK

River
Paved Road
Dirt Road
Put in, Take out

≈ ≈ ≈ CURRANT CREEK

Difficulty: Class 1 to 3.
Length: Up to 30 miles.
Average Gradient: 40 ft./mi,
Season: May, June.
Time: 1 to 2 days.
Character: Transitioning from mountain to desert, mostly continuous steady drop, logs.
Levels: >200 cfs, 2.5 on the gauge just above U.S. 40 is ideal.
Elevation: Put-in below Reservoir 7540 ft., take-out at confluence with Strawberry River 5940 ft.
Topo Maps: Jimmies Point, Raspberry Knoll, Deep Creek Canyon, Fruitland, Strawberry Pinnacles.
Permits: No.
Shuttle Length: Above U.S. 40, same as river length. Below U.S. 40, 9 miles to where Red Creek comes in, 5 more to Strawberry River.
Access: Put-in and take-out are from U.S. 40 east of Strawberry Reservoir. Access the upper part from the road to Currant Creek Reservoir and the lower part from the Red Creek Road (about 7 miles farther east) that goes to Strawberry Pinnacles.

In high-water years, this can be an interesting run. Many years it can't be run at all. Fourteen miles north of U.S. 40, Currant Creek Reservoir offers bathrooms, water, and camping. Starting just below the dam, the river enters a challenging little gorge for a quarter mile. You are then presented with a different kind of challenge: winding your way through miles of willows down to Water Hollow. Below there is the better run. Class 1 and 2 rapids are scattered from there to U.S. 40.

Below U.S. 40 you will see old cars and other junk. As you get farther along, the scenery improves greatly as you meander through ranch land. After several miles a narrower canyon offers some technical Class 2 rapids. It soon opens up to an area with summer homes. You enter a second canyon that continues to where the Red Creek road comes in. The best rapids in this stretch are near the beginning. Even though Red Creek is smaller, the river is called Red Creek after this. A mile of flatwater takes you to a steeper section of Class 2+ to 3- drops near some large pipes. The river continues fast to its confluence with the Strawberry River.

Watch out for logs. If the river is above 2.5 on the gauge at U.S. 40, the last few miles will have some pretty good waves.

≈ ≈ ≈ DIAMOND FORK

Difficulty: Class 1 to 3.
Length: 11 miles.
Average Gradient: 50 ft/mi.
Season: June, July.
Time: 3 to 4 hours.
Character: Steady drop, open canyon and farmland, road along most of it.
Levels: >200 cfs.
Elevation: Put-in 5500 ft., take-out 4950 ft.
Topo Maps: Rays Valley, Billies Mountain, Spanish Fork Peak.
Permits: No.
Shuttle Length: Same as river length.
Access: From U.S. 6 in Spanish Fork Canyon take the Diamond Fork turnoff. The road roughly follows the river, so you can get in and out at many places. The highest put-in is at Three Forks, where almost all the water comes in from Sixth Water.

The first 1.5 miles are fairly steep and narrow Class 2+ to 3. Logs can be a problem. There aren't any major individual drops, just a continuous one. The difficulty gradually eases as you go. The last time I was there, a barbed-wire fence crossed the river just below the bridge to Brimhall Canyon. It was easy to see and possible to sneak under. There are also some bridges and pipes to duck under. Trees can get caught anywhere along this run but are most dangerous near the top because the river is faster. The river may soon be put into a pipe, so enjoy it while you can.

SIXTH WATER

DIAMOND FORK

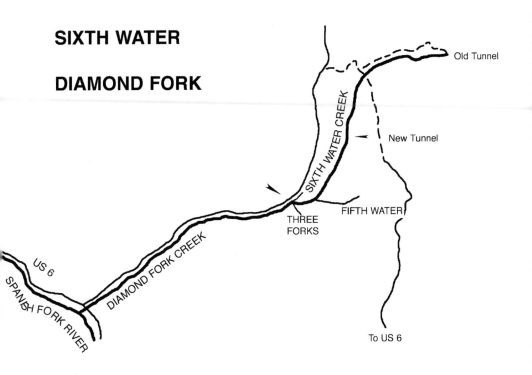

Old Tunnel

SIXTH WATER CREEK

New Tunnel

THREE
FORKS

FIFTH WATER

DIAMOND FORK CREEK

US 6

SPANISH FORK RIVER

To US 6

River	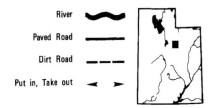
Paved Road	
Dirt Road	
Put in, Take out	◄ ►

Diamond Fork.

≈ ≈ ≈ **DIRTY DEVIL RIVER**

Difficulty: Class 1 to 2.
Length: 83 miles.
Average Gradient: 9 ft./mi.
Season: March-May.
Time: 3 to 5 days.
Character: Spectacular desert canyon, mainly flatwater, shallow, sand
    bottom; watch out for flash floods.
Levels: >100 cfs.
Elevation: Put-in 4240 ft., take-out at Poison Spring 3920 ft., take-out at
    Lake Powell 3700 ft.
Topo Maps: The Notch, Point of Rocks West, Hanksville, Angel Cove,
    Angel Point, Burr Point, Stair Canyon, Hite North.
Permits: No.
Shuttle Length: 53 miles from Hanksville bridge to Hite, 35 miles to
    Poison Spring crossing—15 of which are slow dirt road.
Access: Put in at the bridge on U-24 just north of Hanksville or take
    the dirt road just south of town that goes to the dump. At a junction
    where the dump is left, continue straight and follow to the river. This
    usually has some very sandy spots. This cuts off about 4 miles of
    river. Take out at the Poison Spring Road (about 18 miles south of
    Hanksville on U.S. 95) if you don't want to paddle on Lake Powell.
    This may require four-wheel drive, or at least a low gear and good
    clearance. Otherwise, continue south on U.S. 95 to Lake Powell and
    Hite Marina or other spots in that area.

Muddy Creek and the Fremont River come together near Hanksville just
upstream of the Highway 24 bridge to form the Dirty Devil River. It is
rare to find much water. You're lucky to have 100 cfs. It can be "run" at
this level. Just think of it as an easier way to see the river canyon than
backpacking. Except at very high water, the river is also quite wide and
shallow, making it hard to go very far without having to get out and walk
your boat to a deeper spot. You can save putting up with the worst of
this by cutting off the first 4 miles by taking the dump road.

    At first the scenery is rather plain, but the river gradually cuts
deeper into the rock layers, becoming quite spectacular by around the

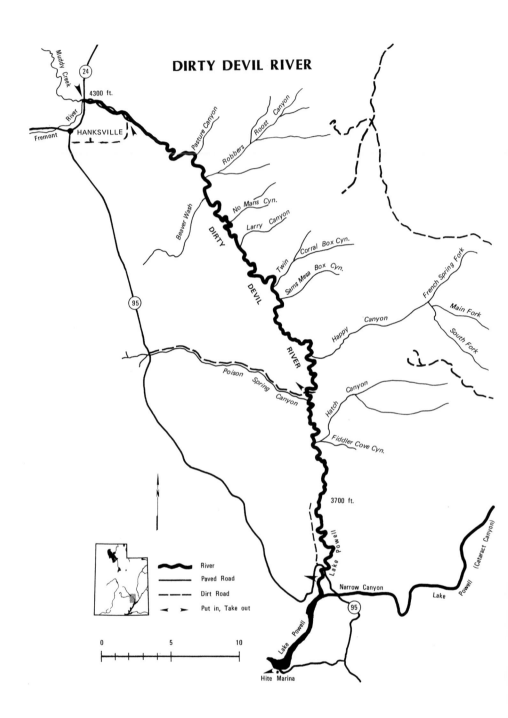

DIRTY DEVIL RIVER

Muddy Creek

24

4300 ft.

River

Fremont

HANKSVILLE

Pasture Canyon

Robbers

Roost Canyon

Beaver Wash

DIRTY

No Mans Cyn.

Larry Canyon

Twin Corral Box Cyn.

Sams Mesa Box Cyn.

DEVIL

French Spring Fork

Main Fork

Happy Canyon

South Fork

RIVER

Poison Spring Canyon

Hatch Canyon

Fiddler Cove Cyn.

3700 ft.

95

N

Lake Powell

Lake Powell (Cataract Canyon)

Narrow Canyon

Lake Powell

95

River

Paved Road

Dirt Road

Put in, Take out

Lake Powell

0   5   10

Hite Marina

"Running" the Dirty Devil River.

lower sand slide, near Buck and Pasture Canyons. The lower sand slide is your last reasonable chance to put in or take out. Below there, the side-canyon hiking becomes outstanding. Robbers Roost is only about 3 miles away. You could easily spend two days hiking just there. About 2 miles past there, on the right is Beaver Canyon, where clear water can often be found. Below, the river makes a huge meander around the Saw Tooth. No Mans Canyon comes in on the left about 7 miles below Robbers Roost. Larry Canyon comes in 4 miles beyond this, again on the left. Eight more miles take you to Twin Corral Box and 1.5 more to Sams Mesa Box, both on the left. Then 9 more miles take you to Happy Canyon on the left with its beautiful narrows a short hike away.

The Poison Spring Canyon road comes in about 8 miles below Happy Canyon. This is one of the few access points. Poison Spring Canyon comes in almost a mile below the road. It's another 12 to 13 miles to Lake Powell if it's full. The water gradually becomes clearer, and all of a sudden you realize you can actually see your paddle when it's in the water. Unfortunately the lack of current means much slower travel. Sometimes you also run into a huge logjam to fight your way through. It is also very likely you will be hit by strong upstream winds, slowing you even more. There are very few places to camp once you hit the lake until you go under Highway 95, where you can take out at the camping area to the right or continue on to Hite.

≈ ≈ ≈ DOLORES RIVER

The Dolores, packed with variety, has one of the longest runs described in this book. At the right water level, you could spend 2 to 3 weeks on it. Unfortunately, the season is somewhat unpredictable due to water being held behind McPhie Dam. Almost always there is at least a short season below where the San Miguel River comes in.

CAHONE (Bradfield Recreation Site) to Slick Rock

Difficulty: Class 1 to 4.
Length: 48 miles.
Average Gradient: 24 ft./mi.
Season: April-June.
Time: 3 days.
Character: Wooded mountain canyon opening into desert by the end, fast current, rocky rapids, minor log problems.
Levels: >900 cfs with rafts, down to about 500 cfs in small craft.
Elevation: Put-in 6460 ft., take-out 5465 ft.
Topo Maps: Doe Canyon, The Glade, Secret Canyon, Joe Davis Hill, Horse Range Mesa, Hamm Canyon, Bull Canyon, Anderson Mesa.
Permits: No, but sign in at put-in.
Shuttle Length: 40 miles.
Access: From Monticello, take U.S. 666 (180) to Cahone. Follow County Road 16 to Bradfield Recreation Site. Take Highway 141 west of Dove Creek to get to Slick Rock.

This stretch is almost totally dependent on releases from McPhie Dam, so there are many years it can't be run. When it can be, it is wonderful. The water is fairly clear and you start in ponderosa pine and work your way to desert. The first few miles below the Bradfield Recreation Site are easy but with continuous small rapids. Beautiful campsites abound. About 15 miles into the trip, you come to Glade Canyon on the right and the canyon makes a major turn left. Several good rapids are in the next mile. The river continues to Mountain Sheep Point. Just before it makes a major bend right are some Indian ruins on the right. After the turn are a pumping station and good rapid.

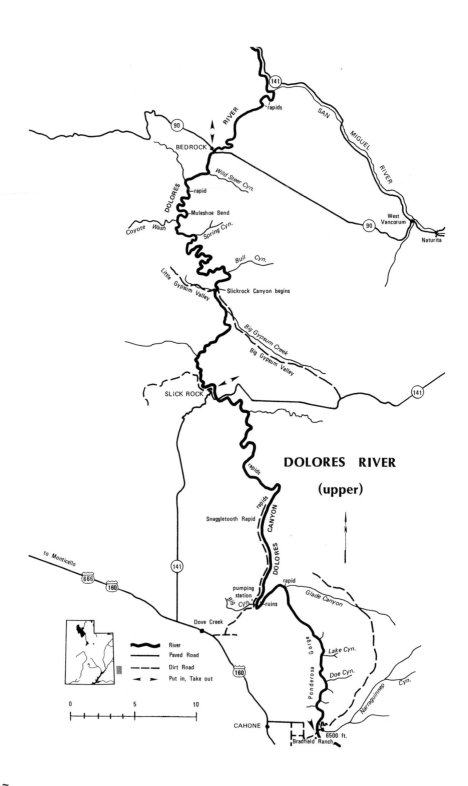

rapids

141

90

BEDROCK

RIVER

SAN

MIGUEL

RIVER

DOLORES

rapid

Wild Steer Cyn.

Muleshoe Bend

Spring Cyn.

Coyote Wash

90

West
Vancorum

Naturita

Bull Cyn.

Little Gypsum Valley

Slickrock Canyon begins

Big Gypsum Creek

Big Gypsum Valley

141

SLICK ROCK

rapids

DOLORES RIVER

(upper)

rapids

Snaggletooth Rapid

CANYON

DOLORES

to Monticello

666

160

141

rapid

pumping
station

Glade Canyon

Big Cyn.

ruins

Dove Creek

160

Ponderosa Gorge

Lake Cyn.

Doe Cyn.

Naraguinnep Cyn.

	River
	Paved Road
	Dirt Road
	Put in, Take out

0   5   10

CAHONE

6500 ft.
Bradfield Ranch

A road comes down Big Canyon on the left, giving access to this section of river. Several rapids are encountered in the next 7 miles. Snaggletooth is about 8 miles below the pumping station. This is the most challenging rapid on this stretch. Depending on water level, it is Class 3+ to 4+, with very high flows creating huge waves and a river-wide hole. Scout this before running. Portaging can be done on the road on the left. The next mile has numerous rapids. About 5 miles below Snaggletooth is Three Mile Rapid, where you will find almost continuous rapids. The river then becomes gentler to Slick Rock. There is a ramp just above the bridge on the right. This is private land. For a small fee, you can park your car by the café.

SLICK ROCK TO BEDROCK

Difficulty: Class 2 to 3.
Length: 49 miles.
Average Gradient: 11 ft./mi.
Season: April-June.
Time: 3 days.
Character: Open valley and then deep slickrock canyon, fairly steady gradient with rapids created by large rocks that have fallen in or been carried in by flash floods.
Levels: >900 except for smaller craft.
Elevation: Put-in 5465 ft., take-out 4950 ft.
Topo Maps: Horse Range Mesa, Hamm Canyon, Anderson Mesa, Paradox.
Permits: No.
Shuttle Length: 60 miles.
Access: Put in from Highway 141 at Slick Rock or at the Gypsum Valley Recreation Site. Get to the take-out by turning off Highway 141 onto Highway 90 and following it to Bedrock.

The river canyon opens up some in the Slick Rock area. The put-in is just above the bridge on river right. Parking is by the café for a small fee. The river flows gently through a short canyon section and on out into Big and Little Gypsum Valleys. Most of the land is private. Most of this section can be bypassed by driving east on Highway 141 to the turnoff for the Gypsum Valley Recreation Site, where you can camp and launch. This

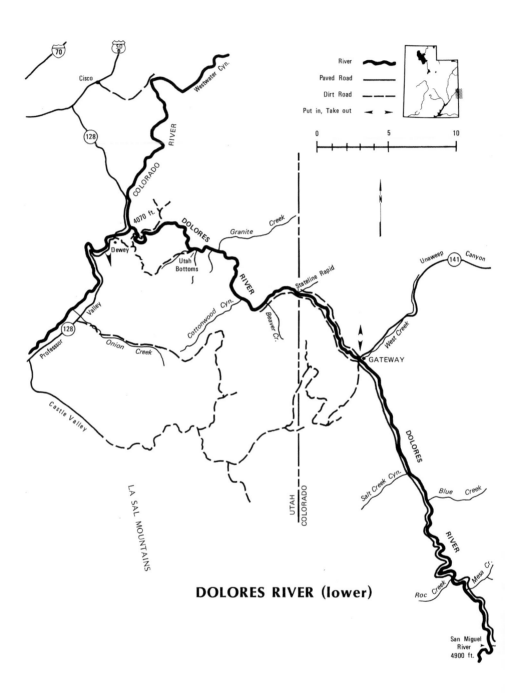

DOLORES RIVER (lower)

involves about 13 miles of dirt road, so it may not save much time over putting in at Slick Rock. About 2 miles below the Gypsum launch site, the river goes under a bridge and enters a beautiful canyon of Wingate Sandstone that you'll be in for the next 33 miles. There are numerous Class≈1 to 3 rapids and outstanding side canyons to hike. There are also occasional petroglyphs on the walls. There are many nice campsites. The takeout is about three-quarters of a mile above Bedrock on river left.

BEDROCK TO GATEWAY

Topo Maps: Paradox, Davis Mesa, Red Canyon, Roc Creek, Juanita Arch, Gateway.

This stretch is about 44 miles long. A side road east of Bedrock follows the river to where the San Miguel River joins. The Dolores River then mostly follows Highway 141. The San Miguel can add a lot of water. When they are not releasing much from McPhie Dam, you can still often run below this tributary. Unfortunately, access is not easy and there is much private land. Put in at the launching area above Bedrock or, according to the "Dolores River Guide" by Ralph DeVries and Stephen G. Maurer, you can put in (with permission from the owner) at private land at Mesa Creek, about 6 miles below the San Miguel. Rapids are Class 2 to 3 but less frequent than sections above.

GATEWAY TO THE COLORADO RIVER

Difficulty: Class 2 to 4+.
Length: 32 miles.
Average Gradient: 13 ft./mi.
Season: April-June.
Time: 2 to 3 days
Character: Open valley to deep desert canyon, isolated, rapids mainly from boulders brought in by flash floods out of side canyons.
Levels: >900 cfs.
Elevation: Put-in 4550 ft., take-out 4090 ft.
Topo Maps: Gateway, Steamboat Mesa, Dolores Point North, Fisher Valley, Blue Chief Mesa, Dewey.
Permits: No.

Beaver Creek Rapid in the Utah stretch of the Dolores River.

Shuttle Length: 120 miles through Grand Junction, 55 miles through Castle Valley.

Access: Put in just above the Highway 141 bridge at Gateway. The take-out by Dewey Bridge can be reached by taking 141 to Grand Junction and then following I-70 to Cisco, where you take U-128 to Dewey Bridge. You could also take the Castle Valley Road to U-128 and then northeast to Dewey Bridge, a rougher but shorter way. I've never tried it but understand you need good maps to avoid getting lost.

About 3.5 miles into the run are some rapids and a diversion dam. You may want to scout this before running. Several more easy rapids follow in the next couple of miles. Two miles of fairly flat water follow this to Stateline Rapid. This is a long and dangerous rapid due to rocks, holes, and logs. It starts with a huge rock in the middle, just above an island. Landing can be a challenge. Scouting from the right is best since this is the side of the island you should run. The next couple of miles offer flat water and good camping.

Beaver Canyon has the second biggest rapid on this section. A big slide a few years ago washed some huge boulders in, changing an easier rapid into a Class 4. There are several nice hikes and camps in the next few miles, along with a few rapids. As the canyon opens up into Utah Bottoms, the wilderness character disappears and a road comes in. The area is rather trashed by those driving off the road. It's about 9 more miles of slower water (one small rapid) to the Colorado River. Part of this has a dirt road along it.

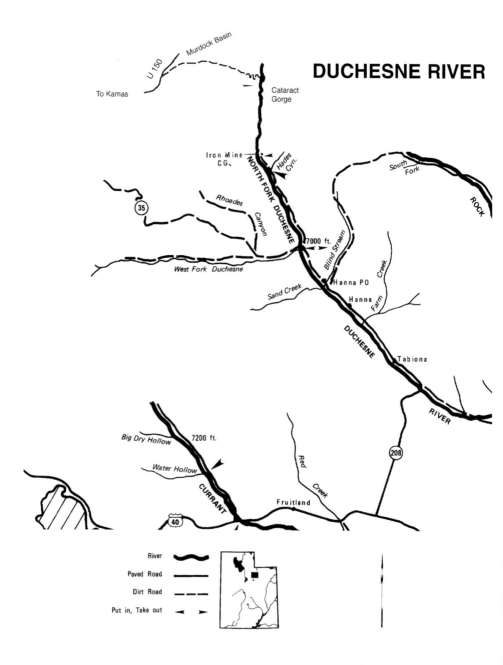

DUCHESNE RIVER

To Kamas

U 150

Murdock Basin

Cataract Gorge

Iron Mine CG.

NORTH FORK DUCHESNE

Hades Cvn.

South Fork

ROCK

Rhoades

Canyon

35

7000 ft.

Blind Stream

West Fork Duchesne

Hanna PO

Sand Creek

Hanna

Farm Creek

DUCHESNE

Tabiona

RIVER

Big Dry Hollow

7200 ft.

Water Hollow

CURRANT

Red Creek

208

Fruitland

40

River

Paved Road

Dirt Road

Put in, Take out

≈ ≈ ≈ DUCHESNE RIVER

Difficulty: Class 2 to 4 (P).
Length: Variable.
Average Gradient: 185 ft./mi. in Cataract Gorge, 62 for N. Fork, 40 for main.
Season: June.
Time: 2 to 5 hours.
Character: Mountain river, small, steep, swift, rocky, great logjam potential. Main Duchesne runs through ranch land with fences and diversion dams.
Levels: Run when the main Duchesne is about 1000 to 1400 cfs.
Elevation: Put-in 8120 ft., take-out 6720 ft. at Hanna.
Topo Maps: Mirror Lake, Iron Mine Mountain, Grandaddy Lake, Hanna, Blacktail Mountain, Talmage.
Permits: No.
Shuttle Length: Cataract Gorge to confluence of North and West Forks is 35 miles by way of Wolf Creek Summit. The rest of the river has roads following, so shuttle is the same length as your run.
Access: Cataract Gorge is reached by taking the Mirror Lake Highway (150) out of Kamas to the Murdock Basin Road. Take the right fork that leads to the East Portal of the Duchesne Tunnel. The rest of the run can be reached from U-35, which goes through Tabiona and Hanna from U.S. 40. You can also get to U-35 from Woodland on the Wolf Creek Road.

NORTH FORK OF THE DUCHESNE RIVER

The first access to the Duchesne River is high in the Uinta Mountains from a dirt road that was built to a diversion tunnel that takes water from the Duchesne River over to the Provo River. You can put in on the little lake formed there. Make sure you get out where the river leaves the lake. A couple waterfalls mark the entrance to Cataract Gorge. Putting in right below the falls is a little tricky. You have to lower your boats down a small cliff, put in on the rocks, and slide into the hardest rapid of the run. If Mark White hadn't been with me the first time we ran this, I'd have put in just below this rapid, but Mark convinced me we'd be fine, and he was right. The river is still steep and continuous after this first rapid for over a mile. It could be hard to stop if a tree were across the river. You may want to scout this first mile before putting in.

As you come out of the gorge, the river eases and splits into several channels, making it hard to find one big enough and clear enough to get through. In about a half-mile you're back to more of a main channel. After a couple miles, the river passes Iron Mine Campground. This is the farthest you can drive up on a public road and thus a possible put-in/take-out point. The next 2 miles to Hades Campground are fairly flat and relaxing. Several Class 1 and 2 rapids will be encountered between there and a small, usually runnable, diversion dam that is about 4 miles up the North Fork and about where the pavement ends. Another diversion dam is about a mile farther down and is more obvious, with cement sides. This diverts water into the Rhodes canal and is easy to walk around. The river joins the West Fork to form the main Duchesne.

MAIN DUCHESNE

The river flows for many miles through farms and past small towns. How far you want to go is up to you, but it also depends on how much water is being taken out along the way. Most years you can count on at least enough to paddle the 7 miles to Hanna. This is also the fastest section, offering Class 1 and 2 paddling. Whatever length you do, watch out for barbed-wire fences, diversion dams, and logs. The last time I paddled to Hanna, there were 3 fences and 2 trees across the river.

The Duchesne River flows on to eventually join the Green River. Below Hanna, the river gradually disappears as it is taken out for agricultural purposes. I have not floated most of this, but I'm not aware of any more major rapids.

≈ ≈ ≈ **EAST CANYON CREEK**

Difficulty: Class 1 to 2.
Length: 11 miles upper, 5 miles lower.
Average Gradient: 45 ft./mi. upper, 60 ft./mi. lower.
Season: Late April, May.
Time: 2 to 3 hours.
Character: Mountain canyon, small, private land, fences, trees, diversion dams.
Levels: 200 to 400 cfs.
Elevation: Put-in 6200 ft., take-out 5700 ft.
Topo Maps: Big Dutch Hollow, East Canyon Reservoir, Porterville, Morgan.
Permits: No.
Shuttle Length: Same as river length.
Access: Take the Jeremy Ranch Exit from I-80. Go to the north side and turn left on the first road (Rasmussen), then turn right on Jeremy Ranch Road and follow it through the housing to where it turns to dirt, and find a place to put in. The road follows the river to U-65 by East Canyon Reservoir. The lower run is right below East Canyon Reservoir along U-66.

JEREMY RANCH TO EAST CANYON RESERVOIR

This stream is only 20 minutes from Salt Lake City. The season is short and usually a little earlier than many of the other rivers in the area. It is almost completely surrounded by private property, so you need to be sure to get in and out at bridges where the main public road crosses. The private land also means fences. There are several scattered throughout the run, so be on your toes. You will also have to pass through a couple pipes. Make sure they are clear before entering. The first half of the run is Class 1 but may require more skill than that to stop for fences, logs, beaver dams, and low bridges. About 1.5 miles above U-65, you pass a red clay bank. From there down, the river is faster Class 2. You could take out when you meet U-65 or continue on through East Canyon Resort and through a pipe where you soon reach East Canyon Reservoir.

You will have to carry your boat a short ways to put in just below the dam. The canyon is fairly narrow, with heavily wooded sections along the river. Many overhanging branches and trees partially or fully block the river. The gradient is fairly steady, so there are no major drops and very few large rocks. Most of the surrounding land is private.

The first mile is the steepest. After the first right bend, you come to an old diversion dam. A cement channel is on the right. Scout this from the put-in road. You can usually run left. About a quarter mile farther is a gauge and a low-head dam. You will probably want to portage. A dirt road comes in there. Below a private picnic area is a short section that is a little steeper and rockier than the rest. Watch out for bridges and fences below there. Take out at the bridge. I haven't run below there. The canyon opens into farmland, so I'm sure there are many fences, bridges, and trees to watch out for.

≈ ≈ ≈ ESCALANTE RIVER

This is a wonderful river with great hiking and camping. Much of it is now free of cattle, so the camping is more pleasant than it used to be. Unfortunately, there often isn't enough water to run the river. When the snowpack is high, though, expect a lot of people to be trying to get on. I wouldn't be surprised if a permit system is put in place sometime in the future. Those who run this river have a special need to practice "Leave No Trace" skills. This is fragile country with a narrow corridor that concentrates use. Please do all you can to leave it better than you found it. Also, be aware that flash floods can occur quickly. Be prepared to move to high ground. I was down there during a thunderstorm when within 10 minutes waterfalls almost as big as the river were pouring off the cliffs. It was an awesome sight. Fortunately, the rain didn't last too long or the river would have been raging.

ESCALANTE TO CALF CREEK BRIDGE (U-12)

Difficulty: Class 1 to 2.
Length: 14 miles.
Average Gradient: 34 ft./mi.
Season: April-June.
Time: 5 to 7 hours.
Character: Beautiful remote desert canyon, shallow, fences, overhanging trees.
Levels: This depends on your tolerance for scraping and walking. It's best if you have at least .3 on the gauge. The flow number should say at least 50 cfs.
Elevation: Put-in 5660 ft., take-out 5200 ft.
Topo Maps: Escalante, Calf Creek.
Permits: Yes, free backcountry permit. Fill out at take-out or stop at Escalante Interagency Visitor Information Center 755 West Main Street (on Highway 12 on the west side of the town of Escalante) or http://www.blm.gov/ut/st/en/fo/grand_staircase-escalante.html. Phone (435) 826-5499.
Shuttle Length: 14 miles.
Access: Put in from the cemetery road just east of the town of

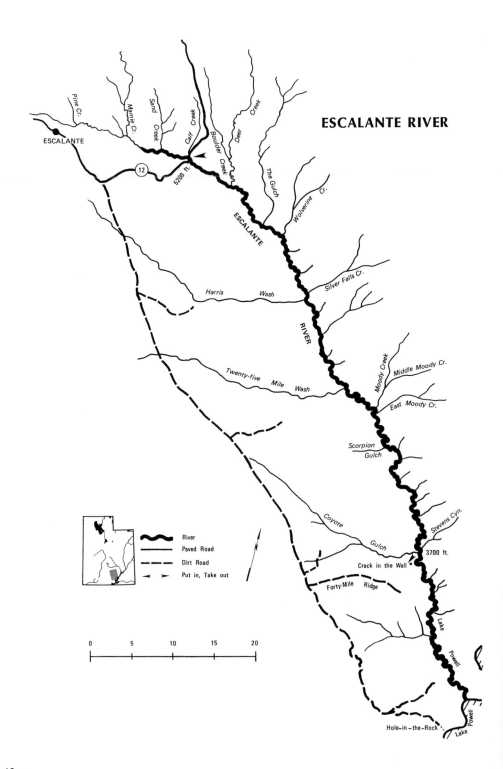

ESCALANTE RIVER

ESCALANTE

Pine Cr.
Mamie Cr.
Sand Creek
Calf Creek
Boulder Creek
Deer Creek
The Gulch
Wolverine Cr.

12

5200 ft.

ESCALANTE

Harris   Wash

Silver Falls Cr.

RIVER

Twenty-five   Mile   Wash

Moody Creek
Middle Moody Cr.
East Moody Cr.

Scorpion
Gulch

Coyote

Gulch

Stevens Cyn.

3700 ft.

Crack in the Wall

Forty-Mile   Ridge

Lake

Powell

Hole-in-the-Rock
Lake Powell

River
Paved Road
Dirt Road
Put in, Take out

0   5   10   15   20

Escalante. You'll have to walk a quarter mile from the end of the road. Take out where the U-12 bridge crosses the Escalante near Calf Creek.

This stretch isn't run often because it's even harder than in the lower section to find sufficient water. When there is enough, you're in for a real treat. Plan on at least 2 hours to Mamie Creek and another 1.5 to 2 hours to Sand Creek. You will then pass an arch and a natural bridge that are easily seen from the river. It's at least another hour from Sand Creek to the take-out by the highway bridge. Watch out for a fence just above the take-out. The gauge is about 50 feet upstream of the bridge on river left.

CALF CREEK TO LAKE POWELL

Difficulty: Class 1 to 3- (P).
Length: 73 miles to Coyote Gulch.
Average Gradient: 20 ft./mi.
Season: April-June.
Time: 5+ days.
Character: Beautiful remote desert canyon, small, shallow, technical boulder gardens in spots.
Levels: This depends on your tolerance for scraping and walking. It's best if you have at least .1 on the gauge. The flow number should say at least 30 cfs. Higher is better.
Elevation: Put-in 5200 ft., take-out 3700 ft.
Topo Maps: Calf Creek, King Bench, Red Breaks, Silver Falls Bench, Egypt, Scorpion Gulch, King Mesa, Stevens Canyon South, Davis Gulch.
Permits: Yes, free backcountry permit. Fill out at take-out or stop at Escalante Interagency Visitor Information Center, 755 West Main Street (on Highway 12 on the west side of the town of Escalante) or http://www.blm.gov/ut/st/en/fo/grand_staircase-escalante.html. Phone (435) 826-5499.
Shuttle Length: Depends on how you get out. From the U-12 bridge to the Hole-in-the-Rock Road is about 9.5 miles. To the 40 Mile Ridge Road is another 35 miles on a dirt road. The last part out to the Crack-in-the-Wall trail is about 5 miles and may require four-wheel drive due to sand. It's another 18.5 miles on the Hole-in-the-

Rock Road to the end if you are getting out that way. The last 5 miles usually require four-wheel drive and high clearance. The drive to Bullfrog Marina via the Burr Trail is about 80 miles and takes about 3 hours.

Access: Put in from U-12 and the bridge by Calf Creek 14 miles east of the town of Escalante. Take out from the Hole-in-the-Rock Road or Bullfrog Marina—see above under Shuttle Length.

This section is usually done in 6 to 7 days. If the water is really high, it could be done in 3 long days, but why? It's too beautiful to just rush through. The lower the water, the more time you need to allow.

The river starts out small. Boulder Creek comes in 6 miles downstream and can sometimes double the flow. Expect some boulders in the river after this, creating some fun rapids for about a mile. The Gulch will also add some water. About a quarter mile below this, on the right just before the river bends left, is a nice spring coming out of the rock just above the river. Horse Canyon is the next major canyon coming in on the left. About 6 miles farther is a grazing allotment fence across the river. You can push through the slats hanging down. No grazing is allowed below there. Silver Falls Creek comes in on the left and then Harris Wash shortly below on the right. Harris often has clear flowing water.

From Harris Wash to Twenty-five Mile Wash are a number of unnamed canyons that are interesting to explore. There is a ruin about a mile up Twenty-five Mile Wash. Continuing on down the Escalante, the next major canyons are on the left, Moody Creek and East Moody being the biggest.

Scorpion Canyon is the next major canyon on the right. If you aren't paying attention, you could miss it. Watch for numerous springs coming out of the right wall in this area. About a mile below, you will start running into large boulders. The first major boulder field looks like it blocks the whole river, but a slot on the right can be run. Expect many more rocks to keep life interesting. When you get to the stretch straight east of the Ezra MC Bench (as seen on the King Mesa Quadrangle), expect to come on a totally blocked section where you will have to portage. This is most easily done on the left. Fools Canyon comes in about 1.5 miles below this on the right. There are often some clear pools there. The last mile or so above Stevens Canyon has limited camping, so take what you can get. The camping is quite poor right at Stevens Canyon. From Stevens to Coyote Gulch, the river is silted in, making it wide and shallow. There is clear flowing water at Coyote Gulch.

Now you have to get out. Either take the hike up Coyote and out Crack-in-the-Wall to the Forty Mile Bench road (plan on a full day for this even though it's only 3.5 miles, and remember that an inflatable kayak is much easier to carry out than a hardshell boat), paddle 25 miles to Hole-in-the-Rock and climb out, paddle 60 miles to Bullfrog, or get a boat pick-up. Boat pick-ups can be arranged at Bullfrog Marina. If you paddle out on Lake Powell and the lake is low, expect up to 6 miles of paddling (walking) through silted-in river below Coyote Gulch. There are numerous springs through this stretch and, at some lake levels, good camping.

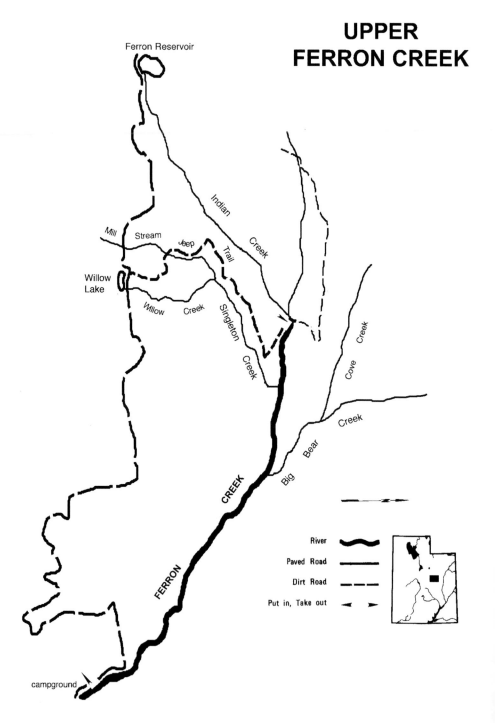

UPPER
FERRON CREEK

Ferron Reservoir

Indian

Mill

Stream

Jeep

Willow
Lake

Willow   Creek

Trail

Singleton

Creek

Creek

Cove   Creek

Creek

CREEK

Big   Bear

FERRON

River

Paved Road

Dirt Road

Put in, Take out

campground

≈ ≈ ≈ FERRON CREEK

UPPER SECTION

Difficulty: Class 3 to 5.
Length: 8 miles.
Average Gradient: 160 ft./mi.
Season: Late May, June.
Time: 5 hours.
Character: Fast, narrow, steep, generally steady gradient, trees, deep
    canyon, remote.
Levels: Around 300 cfs.
Elevation: Put-in 7550 ft., take-out 6500 ft.
Topo Maps: Ferron Reservoir, Ferron Canyon.
Permits: No.
Shuttle Length: 13 miles on the main dirt road and 5 on a jeep road.
Access: Follow Highway 10 to Ferron, turn east on the road to Millsite
    Reservoir. The road turns to dirt but is fine in a passenger car. It fol-
    lows the river for several miles, passing Ferron Canyon Campground.
    This is a good take-out. Continue on the road where it turns left and
    leaves the river to climb fairly steeply up the mountain. At Willow
    Lake turn right and follow a jeep road (need some clearance and a
    low gear) down over Singleton Flat and then left to Ferron Creek to
    put in about where Indian Creek joins.

The window for catching this outstanding run is small. By the time the
snow has melted enough to get into the put-in, the river level is starting
to drop. Ferron Creek cuts a deep narrow gorge through this section.
You're mostly dealing with Class 2 water and an occasional Class 3 to 4
rapid. The trees and gradient, however, require Class 4 to 5 skills. I would
not do this with a group of more than 2 or 3 people. If your group is bigger, break into smaller groups. The "must make" eddies are small and the
turns can be blind. High water would be treacherous. There is one Class 5
section that drops about 20 feet in about 200 feet of river. It looks potentially runnable if trees don't block it. When we were there it was full of
trees. Fortunately, it's fairly easy to stop above. This section down to Big

Bear Creek drops at a rate of about 200 feet per mile. It is only about 2.5 miles, but plan on 3 hours or so to handle scouting and portaging trees.

At Big Bear Creek, the river changes character. The canyon opens a little more, is a little less steep, and there are more boulders. There are fun Class 3 and 4 drops one after the other. It can pretty much be eddy scouted. It's this way for the next 2.5 miles. You can still expect some trees all the way across, but it's easier to stop. The canyon opens up as you pass Steamboat Point and becomes mainly Class 1 and 2 out to Ferron Canyon Campground.

LOWER SECTION

Map: See p. 42.
Difficulty: Class 2 to 3+.
Length: 3.7 miles.
Average Gradient: 75 ft./mi.
Season: May, June.
Time: 1 to 2 hours.
Character: Open canyon, small, fairly steady gradient, a few logs, rocks.
Levels: >250 cfs; 400 to 500 cfs is ideal.
Elevation: Put-in 6500 ft., take-out 6220 ft.
Topo Maps: Ferron Canyon, Flagstaff Peak, Ferron.
Permits: No.
Shuttle Length: About the same as river run.
Access: Follow Highway 10 to Ferron, turn east on the road to Millsite Reservoir. The road turns to dirt but is fine in a passenger car. It follows the river for several miles, passing Ferron Canyon Campground. This is a good put-in. Take out at Millsite Reservoir.

This is a great stretch for the intermediate paddler. The road follows it, so you can put in and take out wherever you want. The river is fairly continuous but only Class 2 for several miles. You do have to watch out for trees, so Class 3 skills are required. It becomes a little rockier and steeper around Birch Creek. The hardest and steepest section (Class 3 to 3+) is the last half-mile, from a little above the National Forest sign down to the gauge, which is right above the reservoir.

Black Canyon of the Bear River.

Cottonwood Creek (Straight Canyon).

Rob Burton on first run of Beaver Creek.

Mark Freed on first run of upper Ferron Creek.

Entrance to Cataract Gorge, North Fork of the Duchesne River.

Escalante River.

Three Fords Rapid in Desolation Canyon of the Green River.

Sand Knolls Rapid in Gray Canyon of the Green River.

Mammoth Creek.

Mark White on first run of upper Provo Falls, a 5-tiered falls.
Photo by James W. Kay, www.jameskay.com

Provo River below Deer Creek Reservoir.

Scrambled Egg Bend on the Weber River.

Sixth Water—Sister Jensen's Green Jell-O Surprise.

Whitewater Park on the Weber River in Ogden.

Willow Creek. Photo by Kirk Nichols.

≈ ≈ ≈ FREMONT RIVER

TORREY TO CAMPGROUND

Difficulty: Class 3 to 6 (P).
Length: 9 miles.
Average Gradient: 130 ft./mi.
Season: March-April.
Time: 6 to 9 hours.
Character: Small, technical, continuous, logs, falls, remote, deep beautiful
   canyon.
Levels: >180 cfs.
Elevation: Put-in 6580 ft., take-out 5420 ft.
Topo Maps: Torrey, Twin Rocks, Fruita.
Permits: No.
Shuttle Length: 13 miles.
Access: For the put-in take Highway 24 to Torrey, then south on High-
   way 12 to where you cross the river. For the take-out go east on
   U-24 to Capitol Reef and take the road past the visitor center to
   where you cross the river by the campground.

This is an incredible section of river. It's hard to find enough water but
not too much. The stretch is only 9 miles but requires a full day to run,
as scouting and portaging are involved. The first quarter mile is quite easy.
The current picks up and carries you past numerous rocks that are quite
a challenge to dodge. Also, watch out for trees and fences. After about a
mile, there will be a couple of sharp turns and then an island splits the
river. This section can be very rocky.

The canyon narrows in another mile. The gradient steepens and several islands cut the flow in half and block the view. From there on proceed carefully, always keeping a place to stop in sight. You will come to
another island with a shallow rocky channel on the left and a 6-foot falls
on the right.

Shortly, the canyon reaches its narrowest point. Some steep rocky
drops should be scouted so that you don't blunder into Hangover Falls.
There the river makes a sharp left and then cuts right and drops 10 to

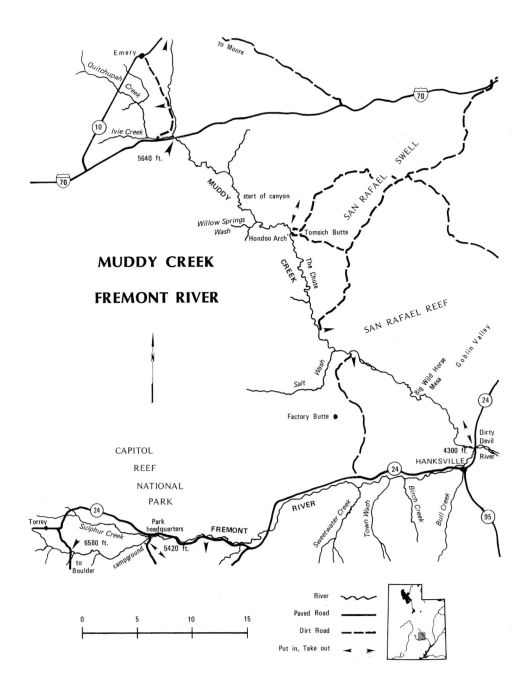

MUDDY CREEK

FREMONT RIVER

15 vertical feet in about the same horizontal distance. Above all this is a huge overhanging boulder. Scout thoroughly before running.

Right after this is a 15-foot vertical waterfall, followed by several more steep drops and falls. The portaging is difficult. A quarter-mile of paddling below all this brings you to another possible portage around a staircase falls hidden around a blind turn. Do not enter this without checking for logs. You may also want to check out the next drop while you're out of the boat.

Not far after this the canyon opens some and becomes less steep. Overhanging brush narrows the river in a few spots, though, creating great potential for a log to get caught. The canyon opens into a little valley at the campground in Capitol Reef National Park.

CAPITOL REEF CAMPGROUND TO WATERFALL

Difficulty: Class 2 to 3.
Length: 7 miles to falls.
Average Gradient: 50 ft./mi.
Season: March-April.
Time: 2 to 3 hours.
Character: Beautiful canyon cutting through Capitol Reef National Park, small, narrow, swift, continuous.
Levels: >180 cfs.
Elevation: Put-in 5420 ft., take-out 5100 ft.
Topo Maps: Fruita, Caineville.
Permits: No.
Shuttle Length: About the same as you paddle.
Access: U-24 follows it.

This section of river runs through the heart of Capitol Reef, offering spectacular views of the slickrock canyon. The road follows the river, so you can put in or take out wherever there is a place to park your car. When the water is high (which is rare), the river is fast and continuous with many small boulders to dodge. There is one undercut spot that can be seen from the road. Make sure you know where the waterfall is so that you don't blunder off it. The landing is not very forgiving. Fast water continues for about a mile beyond the falls and then slows way down and meanders through farmland to where it joins Muddy Creek and becomes the Dirty Devil River.

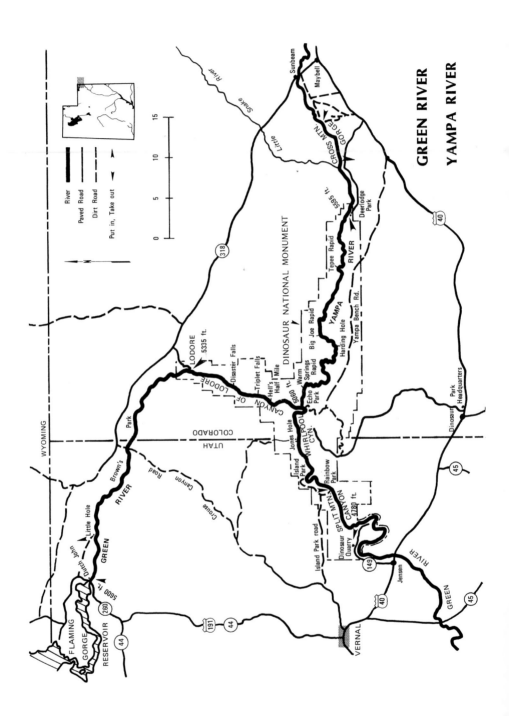

GREEN RIVER
YAMPA RIVER

≈ ≈ ≈ GREEN RIVER

FLAMING GORGE TO LODORE

Belknap's "Dinosaur River Guide" is an excellent map for this section.
Difficulty: Class 1 to 2+.
Length: 7 to 46 miles.
Average Gradient: 14 ft./mi. to Little Hole, 4 ft./mi. after.
Season: All year; can freeze.
Time: 3 hours to 3 days.
Character: To Red Creek is pool drop, flat after that, excellent fishing, great wildlife viewing.
Levels: Any, dam controlled; minimum release is usually 800 cfs.
Elevation: Put-in 5600 ft., take-out 5335 ft.
Topo Maps: Dutch John, Goslin Mountain, Clay Basin, Warren Draw, Swallow Canyon, Lodore School, Canyon of Lodore North.
Permits: No.
Shuttle Length: Varies but usually a few miles longer than the run you pick.
Access: U.S. 191 takes you from Vernal to the Flaming Gorge Dam. After crossing the dam take the road on the right that takes you down to the put-in just below the spillway. To get to Little Hole, continue on U.S. 191 for about 2 miles (just past Dutch John) and turn right and follow 7 miles to the river. For the rest of the access points, continue north on U.S. 191 to the Clay Basin turnoff. Follow this to whichever access point you want. It eventually connects with Colorado Highway 318, which leads to the Gates of Lodore turnoff.

One of the most popular short float trips in Utah is through Red Canyon just below Flaming Gorge Dam. The road to the river drops steeply from the east side of the dam. Parking is limited, and the place is busy. Launch as quickly as possible. If you do this run in a canoe, be aware that extra flotation in the canoe is required.

There are several moderate rapids on the 7-mile run to Little Hole. Trout fishing is world class. A hiking trail follows the east side of the river to Little Hole.

Four miles below Little Hole is Red Creek Rapid, which is rockier and more difficult than any of those above. After another 2 miles of river, you leave Red Canyon and enter Brown's Park. After 2.5 more miles you will come to a BLM boat ramp on the left. Eight more miles of mostly slow water take you through Swallow Canyon, where a BLM boat ramp is found on the left. The river crosses into Colorado 2 miles below.

Enjoy the birds and other wildlife as you slowly float through Brown's Park National Wildlife Refuge, an area named for Canadian trapper Baptiste Brown, who moved there in 1827. Brown's Park, or Brown's Hole as it was originally known, was a refuge for outlaws and rustlers such as Butch Cassidy and the Wild Bunch, into the 1900s. Camping is allowed in designated river campgrounds.

The river enters Dinosaur National Park 1.5 miles above the Lodore ranger station. A permit is required for river travel past the ranger station.

LODORE THROUGH SPLIT MOUNTAIN

Belknap's "Dinosaur River Guide" is an excellent map for this section.
Difficulty: Class 2 to 4-.
Length: 44 miles.
Average Gradient: 14 ft./mi.
Season: All year; can freeze.
Time: 1 to 5 days.
Character: Deep beautiful canyons, remote, pool/drop rapids.
Levels: >800 cfs.
Elevation: Put-in 5335 ft., take-out 4780 ft.
Topo Maps: Canyon of Lodore North, Canyon of Lodore South, Jones Hole, Island Park, Split Mountain, Dinosaur Quarry.
Permits: Yes, year-round. NPS, Dinosaur National Monument, (970) 374-2468, http://www.nps.gov/dino/planyourvisit/privateriverrafting.htm
Shuttle Length: 135 miles.
Access: For the put-in, go east on U.S. 40 and then northwest on Colorado 318 to the Gates of Lodore turnoff. Follow this to the ranger station. Dirt back roads over Diamond Mountain and down Crouse Canyon can also get you there in half the distance but about the same time (impassable when wet). The take-out is near the Dinosaur Quarry at the Split Mountain Campground. Turn north off U.S. 40 at Jensen on U-149 and drive to the campground. To get to the Split

Lodore Canyon of the Green River, Hell's Half Mile.

Whirlpool Canyon of the Green River.

Mountain put-in, take the Brush Creek Road from U-149 and follow the signs to Rainbow Park (can be bad when wet).

A trip through the Canyon of Lodore, Whirlpool Canyon, and Split Mountain takes three days or more. Day trips can be done through Split Mountain. Most people take out at the ramp by the Split Mountain Campground.

The Canyon of Lodore is about 19 miles long. The rapids are fairly frequent and probably the best of any on the Green River, especially at the rare times of high water. Three of the most interesting are Disaster Falls, Triplet Falls, and Hell's Half Mile. The current slams into a large boulder at Triplet. A number of pins have occurred there. Those unfamiliar with Hell's Half Mile may want to make a quick scout. The upper part is the wildest. The river then spreads quite wide in the last part, making it a challenge to get past the many rocks at low water. During spring runoff, the Yampa River greatly enlarges the Green as you enter Echo Park, where you can cool off at Whispering Cave or look at some interesting petroglyphs.

After Echo Park comes Whirlpool Canyon. The rapids aren't as big or as frequent but are still enjoyable. Jones Hole, a popular camping spot, is halfway through the canyon on the right. It offers a refreshing stream with a worthwhile hike along it to some petroglyphs. Don't be surprised if skunks visit you during the night.

Island Park and Rainbow Park will give you plenty of slow water (8 miles) to relax on. Then comes Split Mountain, where the river seemingly took the hard way, cutting straight through the mountain instead of going around it. The river picks up speed and takes you through 8 miles of lively rapids before the take-out at Split Mountain Campground, near the Dinosaur Quarry. The main rapids are Moonshine, S.O.B., Schoolboy, and Inglesby.

Day trips through Split Mountain start at the Rainbow Park boat ramp, which is accessible by way of the road going over Diamond Mountain if coming from Vernal, or by the Brush Creek Road if coming from the take-out.

SPLIT MOUNTAIN CAMPGROUND TO SAND WASH

Topo Maps: Dinosaur Quarry, Split Mountain, Jensen, Rasmussen Hollow, Vernal SE, Brennan Basin, Pelican Lake, Ouray, Uteland Butte, Moon Bottom, Nutters Hole, Duchess Hole.

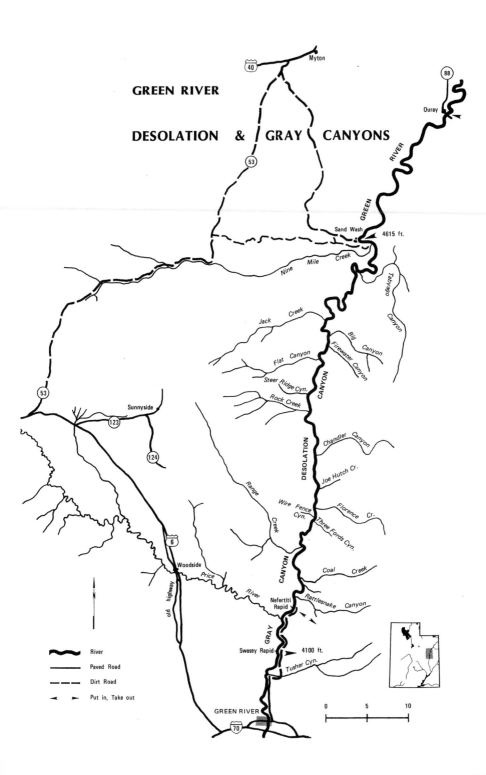

GREEN RIVER

DESOLATION & GRAY CANYONS

Myton

Ouray

GREEN RIVER

Sand Wash   4615 ft.

Nine   Mile   Creek

Tabyago   Canyon

Jack   Creek

Flat   Canyon   Big   Canyon

Firewater Canyon

Steer Ridge Cyn.

Rock Creek

DESOLATION   CANYON

Sunnyside

Chandler   Canyon

Joe Hutch Cr.

Range

Wire   Fence   Cyn.

Florence   Cr.

Three Fords Cyn.

Creek

Coal   Creek

CANYON

Woodside

Price

River

Nefertiti Rapid

Rattlesnake   Canyon

old   highway

GRAY

Swasey Rapid   4100 ft.

Tusher Cyn.

	River
	Paved Road
	Dirt Road
	Put in, Take out

GREEN RIVER

0   5   10

≈ 83

Split Mountain of the Green River.

The first mile or two is still within the boundaries of Dinosaur National Monument and so may require a permit. No permit is needed on the rest. There are a few small rapids and riffles. The river then flattens and slows all the way to Sand Wash. I have run only part of this, but you will mainly be floating through farmland and low hills. Bird life is abundant. Access points include the U.S. 40 bridge (about 18 miles), the U-45 bridge between Naples and Bonanza (about 11 more miles), the bridge at Ouray (about 43 more miles), and Sand Wash (about 34 more miles).

DESOLATION AND GRAY CANYONS

Belknap's waterproof "Desolation River Guide" is an excellent map for this section.
Difficulty: Class 2 to 3.
Length: 85 miles.
Average Gradient: 6 ft./mi.
Season: All year; can freeze.
Time: 4 to 6 days.
Character: Deep remote canyons, pool/drop rapids.
Levels: All, usually ranges from 2000 to 20,000 cfs.
Elevation: Put-in 4615 ft., take-out 4100 ft.

Topo Maps: Duchess Hole, Nutters Hole, Firewater Canyon North, Cedar Ridge Canyon, Chandler Falls, Three Fords Canyon, Butler Canyon, Tusher Canyon.

Permits: Yes, year-round. No permit required below Nefertiti Rapid in Gray Canyon. BLM, Price Resource Area, (435) 636-0975, http://www.blm.gov/ut/st/en/fo/price/recreation/riverinf.html.

Shuttle Length: 185 miles; flying is a great way to do it. Contact BLM.

Access: From U.S. 40, just west of Myton, take the road heading south signed for Sand Wash. At first the road is paved and then it becomes dirt but is usually passable in a car. The last several miles are in a wash and can get rough enough that a vehicle with a little extra clearance can be helpful.

This is a great wilderness stretch, taking you through some of the remotest areas in Utah. The Green River winds out of the Uinta Basin and enters the Tavaput Plateau, creating a gorge that splits the plateau into its east and west halves. This gorge has been known as Desolation Canyon and the lower 36 miles as Gray Canyon (not Gray's) since John Wesley Powell and his men traversed it in 1869 and 1871.

The main put-in for this stretch is at the mouth of Sand Wash. There is a BLM ranger station there along with some interesting old buildings. This was the site of a ferry crossing that was active from about 1920 into the 1950s. The mosquitoes love river runners and will most likely be awaiting your arrival.

The river flows peacefully for the next 26 miles, giving most people plenty of time to acquire painful sunburns if they don't cover up. Small riffles can be found at the mouths of Tabyago Canyon, Rock House Canyon, and Little Rock House Canyon. Starting about a mile above Tabyago Canyon, the Uintah and Ouray Indian Reservation borders the east side of the river for the next 62 miles to the mouth of Coal Creek. Camping on that side requires a permit from the tribe.

Just upstream from the lower Gold Hole, under a cliff on the left, is an interesting old wooden boat with an iron bow. Around the corner from Stampede Flat, on the left, up a side canyon, are some interesting hoodoos. After going around Peters Point, look for an arch partway up the right wall. Light House Rock stands out on the bend about a mile below the arch. The rapids start at Jack Creek. From there on expect a rapid every half mile to mile through Desolation Canyon. The mosquitoes also finally ease off. Firewater Canyon comes in on the left about 4 miles below Jack Creek. The canyon just upstream of Firewater contains an interesting old bootleggers' cabin. The best-known and largest panel of Fremont-style petroglyphs in the canyon is on the right, just upstream from Flat Canyon. Steer Ridge Rapid is usually the most challenging rapid above Rock Creek.

Rock Creek is the cold, clear stream coming in on the right from the 10,000-foot-high ridge of the western Tavaput Plateau. The main canyon is over 5000 feet deep there. Do not use soap in the stream. Camping is not allowed near Rock Creek or at the ranch below. Several old buildings still stand that were built near 1900 by Dan and Bill Seamounton. If you hike about 2 miles up Rock Creek, you can find petroglyphs on the right wall.

Chandler Creek, another cold, clear stream, comes in on the left. A four-wheel-drive road comes in there and continues down to Florence Creek. "No trespassing" signs have been put up fairly recently. Permission from the Indians is required to explore this area. There are petroglyphs and the faint initials "D.J." on some rocks. The initials are thought to belong to Denis Julien, a French-Canadian trapper who traveled these canyons in the 1830s. A stone chimney from a house thought to have been built by Joe Hutch, an early settler, is also in the area.

The rapids at Chandler Creek, Joe Hutch Creek, and Joe Hutch Canyon are the most challenging rapids in this section. About a mile below Joe Hutch Canyon, on the east side, is Florence Creek Lodge. Behind this are the old McPherson Ranch buildings. In 1942, the U.S. government bought the McPherson Ranch from the Wilcox family to add to the Indian reservation. Then the lodge was built. You may or may not be welcome if you stop to see this area. Some years there have been signs welcoming boaters, with cold drinks available to buy. Some years there have been "no trespassing" signs. And some years there have been no signs at all.

After the wider valley of the McPherson Ranch, the Green River starts cutting through the Flagstaff Limestone, a grayer rock. This happens in the Wire Fence area and marks the beginning of Gray Canyon. The rapids in Gray Canyon are generally separated by longer stretches of flat water, but the drops are usually steeper and longer. Campsites become less frequent.

Wire Fence Rapid was made more exciting a few years ago when a flash flood brought in large boulders that squeezed the river much tighter, creating a short steep drop. Right around the bend is Three Fords Rapid. This is one of the most challenging of the entire run.

About 6 miles below Three Fords is Range Creek Rapid. This often has fairly large waves on the left. Another 5 miles and 3 rapids take you to Coal Creek Rapid, one of the rockiest rapids in these canyons. It's fairly hard to scout. There are holes and rocks to dodge. Near the end of it, on the left, are the ruins of some stone houses left from an attempt to dam the Green River there in 1911. Rattlesnake Rapid is another 3 miles away. Camping spots between Coal Creek and Rattlesnake are in high demand, as everyone wants to spend their last night above where the road comes in.

The road from the town of Green River comes up to just above Nefertiti Rapid, offering a put-in or take-out point on river left. This is the beginning of the "daily" section. The Price River comes in 2 miles farther down. Five more rapids are encountered below the Price River and above Swasey Beach, the most popular take-out. They are Butler, Sand Knolls, Stone House, Short Canyon, and Swasey Rapids. Small boats can take out at the beach but larger boats are more easily taken out at the ramp on the bend. There are several bathrooms at access points along the "daily" stretch and a campground with garbage pick-up at Swasey Beach.

Should you decide to float to the town of Green River, be aware that 3 miles below Swasey there is a diversion dam with bad hydraulics, immediately followed by Tusher (or Pumphouse) Rapid. Eight more miles of flat water take you to Green River State Park.

GREEN RIVER STATE PARK TO COLORADO RIVER
(Labyrinth and Stillwater Canyons)

Belknap's waterproof "Canyonlands River Guide" is an excellent map for this section.
Difficulty: Class 1.
Length: 121 miles.
Average Gradient: 1.4 ft./mi.
Season: All year.
Time: 3 to 6 days.
Character: Deep desert canyons, wide smooth river.
Levels: All; usual range is from 2000 to 20,000 cfs.
Elevation: Put-in 4050 ft., take-out 3900 ft.
Topo Maps: Green River, Horse Bench East, Green River SE, Tenmile

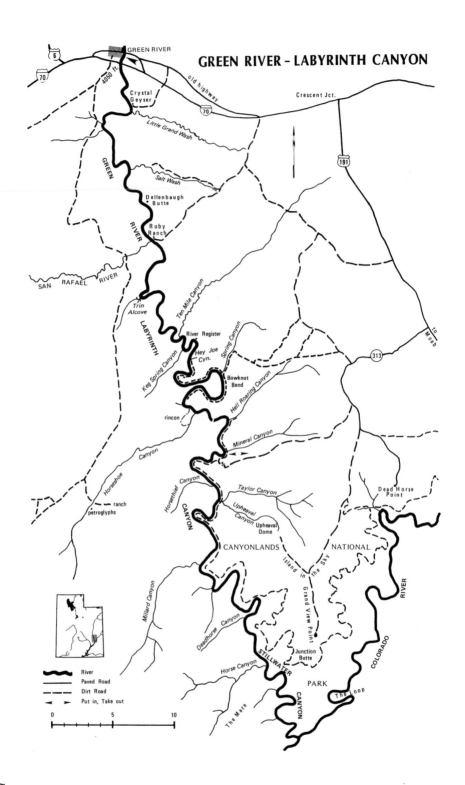

GREEN RIVER - LABYRINTH CANYON

GREEN RIVER

Crescent Jct.

old highway

Crystal Geyser

4050 ft.

Little Grand Wash

GREEN

Salt Wash

Dellenbaugh Butte

RIVER

Ruby Ranch

SAN RAFAEL RIVER

Trin Alcove

LABYRINTH

Ten Mile Canyon

River Register

Spring Canyon

Keg Spring Canyon

Hey Joe Cyn.

Bowknot Bend

Hell Roaring Canyon

to Moab

313

rincon

Mineral Canyon

Canyon

Horseshoe Canyon

Horsethief Canyon

Taylor Canyon

Dead Horse Point

ranch
petroglyphs

CANYON

Upheaval Canyon

Upheaval Dome

CANYONLANDS

NATIONAL

Island in the Sky

RIVER

Millard Canyon

Grand View Point

Deadhorse Canyon

Junction Butte

COLORADO

STILLWATER

Horse Canyon

PARK

The Loop

CANYON

The Maze

River
Paved Road
Dirt Road
Put in, Take out

0   5   10

Point, Bowknot Bend, Mineral Canyon, Horsethief Canyon, Cleopatras Chair, Upheaval Dome, Turks Head, Spanish Bottom.

Permits: Not at this time unless you go below Mineral Bottom. BLM (435) 636-3622. Check web site for other requirements: http://www. blm.gov/ut/st/en/fo/price/recreation/labyrinth.html. For boating below Mineral Bottom you must get a permit. NPS, Canyonlands National Park, (435) 259-4351, http://www.nps.gov/cany/planyourvisit/rivers.htm.

Shuttle Length: 74 miles to Mineral Bottom (18 of which are dirt), 50 miles to Moab (if jet boating up to Moab).

Access: Green River State Park is the most common put-in. From I-70, take the Green River exit. In the town of Green River, look for the sign for the state park. They charge a fee to launch and to leave a vehicle. Camping, water, and bathrooms are available there. To put in at Ruby Ranch, go east on I-70 to the ranch exit and follow the dirt road south to the ranch. They charge a higher fee than the state park. To get to Mineral Bottom, go east on I-70 to the Moab turnoff (U.S. 191), then go about 20 miles to the Canyonlands and Dead Horse Point turnoff (U-313). Follow this about 12 miles to the signed dirt road to Mineral Bottom. Follow the dirt road about 18 miles. Enjoy the spectacular switchbacks down to the river. At the bottom of them, make sure you stay right (left goes to the White Rim Trail) and head upstream to the launching area. There is a ranger station and bathroom there but no water.

This is probably the best canoe camping section of river in the state. At this time, no permits are required. It has become very popular, so don't expect to have the canyon to yourself. Please follow "Leave No Trace" principles. Toilets are required. Leave your campsite better than you found it. Memorial weekend is still the time of the Friendship Cruise, when powerboats roar down the Green River and up the Colorado River to Moab.

Camping can be a challenge due to the dense growth of tamarisk—a non-native species. Look for sandbars or a way to get behind the tamarisk, usually found at the beginning or end of a "bottom." Mosquitoes and biting flies can be severe problems at times, so come prepared. Almost all the side canyons have interesting hikes, so allow some time to explore. Don't expect to find much clear flowing water. It's best to bring your own.

Labyrinth Canyon of the Green River.

There are several riffles in the first 12 miles. After that the river is quite smooth. About 4.5 miles from the state park you will see some orange-colored rock on the left. Crystal Geyser is at the top of this. A couple times a day, carbon dioxide builds enough pressure to set this cold-water geyser off. It can shoot as high as 60 to 70 feet and last for 20 minutes.

The San Rafael River comes in on the right across from Ruby Ranch. The ranch can be used as a launching point for a fee. Stop in at the house to pay. This cuts off about 23 miles of river but adds more dirt-road driving. Labyrinth Canyon starts about 4 miles below the ranch. Three more miles take you to Three Canyon (Trin-Alcove). This is a popular hiking and camping spot.

The River Register is a spot just past mile 78 (in the Belknap guide) where modern man has carved his name along with some interesting pictures. Unfortunately, many of the early inscriptions have now been written over. These were unique and rare. With thousands of people going down each year, your inscription is neither. Please don't write on the wall. Sign the paper register that is in the ammo can if you feel the need to do so.

A little over a mile below the register is Hey Joe Canyon on the left.

A rough dirt road comes from Spring Canyon up to the old uranium mines there. A faint Denis Julien inscription, "16 Mai 1836," is located about 1.5 miles below there on the left, shortly above the high-water mark. Julien was a French-Canadian trapper in the area. He was an old man by the time he was there and may have been the first white person to take a boat down the Green River. A mile farther is another inscription, "Launch Marguerite 1909." This was the name of a steamboat used briefly on the river.

The saddle at Bowknot Bend is reached in another 3 miles. The river travels about 6 miles to arrive a quarter of a mile away. A short steep hike takes you to the saddle from either side. A number of inscriptions are found there. Again, please don't add yours. Use the register partway across the saddle. As you go around Bowknot Bend, you will see many uranium mines. Many of these were active into the 1980s. You will pass Spring Canyon, where the road comes in that goes up and down the river to these mines.

On the right, about 2 miles past Oak Bottom, is Horseshoe Canyon. The lower end is a "rincon," a cut-off meander of the river. When the river broke through there, it saved you about 2 miles of paddling. Shortly below this, on the right, is a 1914 inscription that includes some names of a U.S. Reclamation Service survey crew. Similar inscriptions may be seen at Bowknot Bend and near the lower D. Julien inscription. His lower inscription, dated "1836 3 Mai," can be seen along with some drawings 200 yards up Hell Roaring Canyon. A road follows the river from there to the most common take-out at Mineral Bottom, approximately 68 miles from the town of Green River.

If you wish to continue downriver, you will need a boat pick-up once you reach the confluence to take you up the Colorado River or the ability and permit needed to run Cataract Canyon. The river continues much as it has been; slow with beautiful scenery. You enter Canyonlands National Park in 5 miles. A permit is required beyond there. You can find ruins at Fort Bottom and Turks Head. A number of side canyons come in, offering many hiking possibilities. You leave Labyrinth Canyon and enter Stillwater Canyon at roughly Anderson Bottom. Once you get to the confluence, it's 3 miles downstream to Spanish Bottom, where you are most likely to be picked up if jet boating up to Moab. Cataract Canyon starts just below.

≈ ≈ ≈ HUNTINGTON CREEK

This steep mountain stream and the Left Fork have some of the finest challenging paddling in the state. At high water, they're fast and pushy. Great care must be taken to avoid logs. This usually means scouting everything you are going to run. At lower flows, much of it becomes more intermediate in difficulty. Scouting can often be done on the fly.

Map: See. p. 42.

LEFT FORK

Difficulty: Class 3 to 4+.
Length: 6.5 miles.
Average Gradient: 135 ft./mi.
Season: Late May, June.
Time: 1 to 4 hours.
Character: Steep, continuous, mountain stream, rocks, logs.
Levels: >200 cfs.
Elevation: Put-in 8360 ft., take-out 7640 ft.
Topo Maps: Candland Mountain, Rilda Canyon.
Permits: No.
Shuttle Length: 16 miles.
Access: Highway 31 from Fairview to Huntington passes the side road going a short distance up the canyon to the Forks of Huntington Campground. This is a good take-out, or get out along the highway. To get to the put-in for the Left Fork, from U-31, take the dirt road (usually passable in a passenger car) between Cleveland and Huntington Reservoirs and follow it to Miller Flat Reservoir. Take the road around the north side of the reservoir.

The Left Fork is an incredible run. It has waterfalls, sloping ledges, blind turns, terrific scenery, and, unfortunately, logs. I first heard about this from someone who had hiked the trail along it. They thought it might interest me. I could never catch it with enough water until one time I was passing by on my way to paddle another river. It was booming, and I scrapped my other plans and ran it.

David Gibson dropping the falls leading into the Left Fork of Huntington Creek.

I recommend putting in from Miller Flat Reservoir. Carry your boat to the first place you can put in on Miller Flat Creek. This tributary to the Left Fork is very tiny. The best falls of the run is just before reaching the Left Fork. The first drop is about 10 feet, followed almost immediately by a 4-foot falls. We found you could run these almost anywhere, but you should scout first. You could also put in from the next canyon upstream (Staker Canyon), which is where the trail for the Left Fork starts. You would have to carry your boat for a half mile or more. Not far below where you would put in is a boulder sieve where rocks have blocked the whole river. Make sure you know where this is and can stop above it. Shortly after it is the junction with Miller Flat Creek.

After this confluence there are two more runnable falls before the river swings left and enters a narrower canyon. There are numerous steep drops. Scout often, as they sometimes are plugged with trees below the horizon line. Some of the trees look quite permanent. All the drops can be run if they are clear. Many are long sloping ledges where you accelerate down and then slam into a pool at the bottom. The lower part is a little easier with easier portaging conditions as well. You can get out at the campground or continue another half mile to the main river.

Huntington Creek.

Huntington Creek

Difficulty: Class 3 to 4+.
Length: Up to 15 miles.
Average Gradient: 110 ft./mi.
Season: Late May, June.
Time: 1 hr. to all day.
Character: Steep, continuous, mountain stream, rocks, logs.
Levels: >250 cfs.
Elevation: Put-in 7640 ft., take-out 6400 ft.
Topo Maps: Candland Mountain, Rilda Canyon, Hiawatha, Red Point.
Permits: No.
Shuttle Length: About the same as river run.
Access: Highway 31 from Fairview to Huntington follows the river, allowing access at almost any point.

The best boating starts where the Left Fork comes in. Scout thoroughly, especially at high water. Much of this can be done from the road, but several of the harder spots can't be seen. At high water the Class 3 to 4+ rapids are quite continuous with few eddies. Class 5 skills may be needed to avoid trees. Lower flows drop the difficulty to Class 2 to 3+, offering many more chances to stop if needed. At the Birch Spring area the river slows down and meanders some, catching many fallen trees.

Below this park-like area, the river goes smoothly away from the road. Just out of sight, you start to plunge down a steeper section and suddenly you are in one of the hardest rapids. We call this "Crooked Elbow" rapid due to an injury on the first run on one of the rocks there. This lasts for about a half mile and then eases somewhat as you come to the Bear Creek Campground. Below this are some tight turns and large boulders; then the water backs up behind a Utah Power dam that is a definite portage.

A mile of excellent rapids immediately follows the dam. The river eases as you come to a bridge leading to the power plant. We usually take out there. If you continue on, watch out for a fence just after the river turns left upon running into the hill below the power plant. It's the kind of fence with pipes freely hanging into the water. As the creek cuts back to the road, it becomes more channeled and eases to Class 2. Still swift in high water, it enters farmland from there on. Watch for low pipes. There is one last steeper section of Class 3 difficulty the last half mile above mile marker 43. After this expect diversion dams and slower water.

JORDAN RIVER
BIG & LITTLE COTTONWOOD CREEKS
AMERICAN FORK RIVER

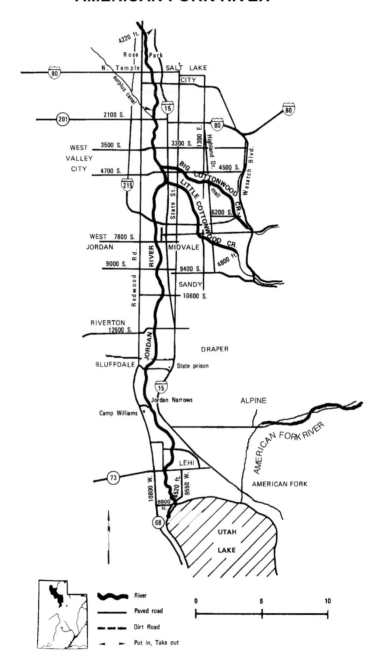

≈ ≈ ≈ JORDAN RIVER

Difficulty: Class 1 to 3 (P).
Length: 56 miles.
Average Gradient: <1 ft./mi. up to 32 ft./mi.
Season: Any.
Time: 1 hour to several days.
Character: Mostly open farmland, generally slow meandering river with a
  few swift sections, fence and dam hazards, great for bird life.
Levels: All but the lowest levels.
Elevation: Utah Lake 4520 ft., Rose Park 4220 ft.
Topo Maps: Saratoga Springs, Jordan Narrows, Midvale, Salt Lake City
  South, Salt Lake City North, Farmington.
Permits: No.
Shuttle Length: Varies depending on section, but there are many access
  points, so shuttles are usually about the same as the length you paddle.
Access: Almost any exit off I-15 between Lehi and 1000 North in Salt
  Lake City will cross the river if you head west. Redwood Road also
  offers good north/south access. Take almost any road off it heading
  east to get to the river. Check out http://www.recreation.slco.org/
  parks/html/locations.html.

Most people still picture the Jordan River as a rat-infested open sewer. It
still has a strange smell to it, but so do most shallow muddy rivers. It's not
a place I'd want to swim, but it actually is far cleaner than it used to be and
has some very beautiful sections. Water levels fluctuate depending on irrigation demands and snowpack. Some years all sections can be run all year. At
other times, only certain sections will have enough water. Many cities along
the way have developed parks and parkways along it. Others are working
on that. The progress is quite slow, but eventually there will be parkway
along most of its length.

UTAH LAKE TO THE NARROWS

The Jordan River is smooth and slow all the way to the Narrows, so it's
great for total beginners. There is good access near Utah Lake at Inlet Park
or R.C. Model Port. From S.R. 73, turn south at 9550 West to get there. The

Jordan River.

river runs about 3 miles from the lake to S.R. 73. There is a paved trail
along it, so you could walk or bike your shuttle. The next access point is 2
miles farther at 9600 North (milepost 35 on Redwood Road). If you go beyond there, you have about 4 miles to the Narrows, where you have access
and trespass problems. As you approach Camp Williams (above the Narrows), the river is constricted by steep hills that replace the open river bottom. You will go under a small bridge. This is where the bike trail turns
around. The river is soon blocked by a cable and fence of logs just before
the dam at the Narrows. Once you arrive there, you have no choice other
than trespassing, unless you have a motor to take you back upstream. Private companies own the land on the left. The railroad owns the land on the
right. Courts throughout the country have generally sided with boaters
when it comes to trespassing in order to get around a hazard such as a
dam or fence, but be aware there could be legal consequences. The right
side is probably the better side to portage. Just don't get in the way of a
train. It takes about 3 hours to paddle from Utah Lake to the Narrows.

THE NARROWS

The Narrows is not for beginners. The water is swift; there are low bridges and dams, overhanging trees and bushes, and a fair amount of maneuvering. Access has been closed mainly because beginners got into trouble and had to be rescued. Some nearly died. Make sure there is water at the Bluffdale road (14600 South) or you might arrive at the lower dam and find out almost all the water is diverted there.

Just north of Camp Williams on Redwood Road, a sign for the pumping station marks the road down to the Narrows (also the turnoff for the Veterans Memorial Park). A dam blocks the river and splits the water into three channels, the center one being the river and the other two canals that go out to farms. Unfortunately, there is no legal access anymore. You can try getting permission or put in on the section previously described.

Shortly below the dam is a gauge and low footbridge. The river is quite fast and exciting, with overhanging bushes and some actual rapids. About a mile below the dam is a play wave that is accessible from the frontage road to I-15. A side road from this goes to a diversion dam. The play spot is just upstream from this lower dam. You will have to portage around the dam to continue. There is a rapid section right after going under the train bridge. There's a small rocky drop just before the river makes a major turn left. After the turn, the river splits. The left was the better channel when I was last there, as the right had a fence across it. You will arrive at 14600 South about a half mile below this. Allow 1.5 to 3 hours to run this 4-mile stretch, depending on water level and playtime.

BLUFFDALE ROAD TO 7800 SOUTH

This section is about 11 miles long, running peacefully through farmland, golf courses, and homes. The fastest water is in the Bluffdale area. It usually takes about 3 hours for this stretch. Several other roads can be used for access: 12600 South, 10400 South, and 9000 South. Home construction and other work could alter this stretch. There also are plans to put back the meanders in the river that used to be there between 9000 South and 7800 South. Some years there have been barbed-wire fences. A diversion dam about a half mile above 9000 South must be portaged.

7800 SOUTH TO 2100 SOUTH

This 11-mile section can usually be run year-round and takes 3 to 4 hours. The parkway is fairly well developed along most of this stretch, so there are paths and bathrooms available. You will need to walk around a dangerous drop at 6400 South. Portage left. A river-wide hydraulic is created as the river pours off a cement pad. It would be easy to be trapped and drown if you went off this drop. Shortly after passing under 4800 South, the river slows as it backs up behind a dam. You can portage on the left. The river slows by the time you get to 3500 South.

Just before 2100 South, you will go under the 201 freeway. You will need to get out at 2100 South. Just below, the actual river goes into pipes for a short distance. What looks like the river goes off an innocent-looking but dangerous drop and becomes the surplus canal. Do not get out on the east side of the river north of 2100 South as this is private land and the owner doesn't welcome boaters. Get out upstream (south) of 2100 South. If you are going to continue on you will have to walk along the west side (by the golf course) of the river past the diversion dam, paddle across the surplus canal, and get back in the river from the west side.

1700 SOUTH TO ROSE PARK

You can put in for this stretch at Raging Waters or at the park across the street. It will take 1.5 to 3 hours to paddle the 4 miles to North Temple. It's about 3 more miles to where Redwood Road crosses the river. There are numerous parks and trails along this whole stretch. The water is generally slow, with many overhanging trees making this a beautiful stretch. It's fairly easy to get pushed into one of the overhanging trees, though, and tipped over. The International Peace Gardens, at about 1000 South, directly adjoins the river and is worth a visit. There is a park and access at 800 South and access from a side street at 300 South.

At about South Temple, you'll encounter a diversion dam for the Utah Power plant. A canoe flume has been built there, supposedly easing the drop for boaters. There is a dock at the Fairgrounds just past North Temple, another at about 300 North behind the Department of Agriculture building, and access at 700 North and 1000 North. You then go through the Rose Park Golf Course and come to Redwood Road at about 1800 North. Most people stop somewhere prior to there. You could continue to Cudahy Lane. Going beyond there gets you out into the Great Salt Lake marshes where there is no access.

≈ ≈ ≈ **LAKE FORK**

Difficulty: Class 2 to 5.
Length: 1.6 miles upper, 6.2 miles lower.
Average Gradient: 200 ft./mi., 67 ft./mi.
Season: June.
Time: 2 to 4 hours.
Character: Steep, narrow, rocky, logs.
Levels: >300 cfs.
Elevation: Put-in 7960 ft., take-out 7125 ft.
Topo Maps: Lake Fork Mountain, Mountain Home.
Permits: No.
Shuttle Length: Roughly the same as river.
Access: From Duchesne and U.S. 40, take U-134 north to Mountain
    Home. Follow the signs to Moon Lake. Put in just below the lake.

Lake Fork has some challenging whitewater below Moon Lake. The first
quarter mile is Class 2+ to 3 with some fairly tight maneuvering and
good gradient but no major drops. A little above the gauge, the river
swings right and makes some short drops through boulders and then
funnels into a narrow 4-foot drop. There is a wicked reversal at really
high water, so scout this. A short flat section separates this from the
steep and challenging triple drop at the gauge. A dirt road comes down
to there. Scout this whole section, especially at high water. It's Class 4 to
5. You get a short break and then a straight boulder section. The river
cuts sharply left and narrows as you enter the third hardest rapid. It's
longer than the other two but not as steep.

    The rapids ease some but are still continuous and rocky. A diversion
dam puts water into the Farnsworth Canal, so you'll have to get out. A
road comes into there from the main road just above two old collapsed
log cabins and below Raspberry Draw. I suggest driving from there for
2 miles to avoid a nightmare of logs.

    Go below the beaver ponds but above the big hill on the east side
of the road. Look for a short side road to the river. Topographical maps
show Lake Fork Corral there. Putting in there gives you about 1.5 miles
of easy paddling with beautiful scenery. Then, once past the cliffs on the

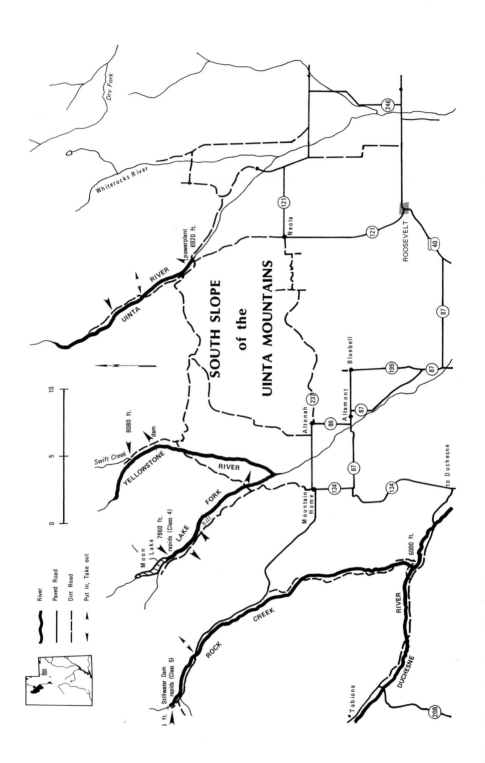

SOUTH SLOPE
of the
UINTA MOUNTAINS

right, there is one rapid after another all the way to the bridge going to the Yellowstone River. The banks through this lower section are bushy, making it difficult to stop at high flows. The river also splits into smaller channels in several places. The potential for logjams is great, but most trees get caught in the slow section above. The bridge is a good take-out.

≈ ≈ ≈ LITTLE COTTONWOOD CREEK

Map: See p. 96.
Difficulty: Class 2 to 4 (P).
Length: 7 miles.
Average Gradient: 70 ft./mi.
Season: May, June.
Time: 3 to 4 hours.
Character: Small, tight, steep above the I-215 crossing, dams, low
    bridges, trees, private property.
Levels: 200 to 500 cfs.
Elevation: 5360 ft. at mouth of canyon, 4240 ft. at Jordan River.
Topo Maps: Draper, Sugar House, Salt Lake City South.
Permits: No.
Shuttle Length: About the same as river run.
Access: 9400 South and Wasatch Blvd. Both offer access to the mouth
    of Little Cottonwood Canyon. Other streets are listed below.

As far as I know, very little in the canyon has been run. Mark White and
Brian Smoot were the first I know of to run the bottom mile or two
back in the 1980s. Mark and Rolf Schindler also ran about 1.5 miles above
White Pine a couple years ago. The bottom mile, from the private side
road with a Wasatch Resort sign down to the Temple Quarry Trailhead at
the mouth of the canyon, has a biking/jogging trail roughly following it,
making access easier. Walk it before you run to check for logs. Lower
water levels are easier. From the mouth of the canyon to Creek Road
there are some dangerous drops, and boating is not recommended there.

The next part that is runnable starts by the intersection of Creek
Road (8145 South) and Water Vista Way (2680 East). There is a double
drop there. In about a quarter mile you go under a low bridge followed
in about 100 feet by a 6-foot drop. There are many more drops before
you come to I-215. All these should be scouted to determine whether
you can run them or not. At I-215, the center chute is probably best.
After that you encounter two more drops before the creek backs up in a
pond behind a dam with a large metal gate. It drops from there in 3 tiers.
Portage. Watch for barbed-wire fences at Wheeler Farm. After this there
are two sections close together where you are funneled between cement

walls with interesting drops where you can't stop, so scout first. After the bridge at 6000 South there is a small drop. You then enter a beautiful stretch past some large homes and some high bluffs, then through many condos and under 5300 South into Murray Park. At really high water you may not fit under some bridges. After going under State Street, the creek goes through a double set of round metal pipes, followed by a small diversion dam near some slag-looking rock. The river goes under I-15 in a double tunnel. It empties into the Jordan River just south of 4800 South.

≈ ≈ ≈ **LOGAN RIVER**

The Logan River offers something for every paddler. You've got great park and play, long mellow stretches for relaxing in a canoe, intermediate white-water sections, and some steep pushy advanced paddling. It's all offered in a beautiful setting with easy access. Utah State University Kayak Club, http://www.usu.edu/canoe.

Map: See p. 19.

LOGAN CANYON—RICK'S SPRING TO THIRD DAM

Difficulty: Class 2 to 3+.
Length: 12.6 miles.
Average Gradient: 70 ft./mi.
Season: May, June.
Time: 3 to 4 hours.
Character: Steep, rocky, narrow, brushy, low bridge, logs, beautiful
    mountain canyon.
Levels: >300 cfs.
Elevation: Put-in 5840 ft., take-out 5020 ft.
Topo Maps: Temple Peak, Mt. Elmer.
Permits: No.
Shuttle Length: About the same as run.
Access: From I-15 take the U.S. 89 exit and go past Brigham City to Logan.
    Turn right in Logan to continue on U.S. 89 up through Logan Canyon.

This is a clear, fast-dropping mountain stream. Since the road follows the river, you can put in and take out wherever you want. This also makes scouting easy.

The most common put-in is at Ricks Spring, just past milepost 390. From there to Preston Valley Campground is fairly constant Class 2 to 3+ with few eddies and lots of overhanging bushes. About a quarter mile from the spring is a steep section called the Slippery Slide. Four miles of busy whitewater takes you to the hardest rapid in this section. It's about a quarter mile above where the road crosses the river (about three-quarters of a mile above milepost 385). A big boulder blocks the middle of the river followed by a short steep drop with several rocks just under the surface. Some good waves follow. The river continues swift and rocky to below Preston Valley Campground. There is a good surf wave at the right level just above the campground.

About a half mile below Preston Valley Campground is a usually runnable diversion dam. Some water is diverted into side tunnels and then dumped back in after about 100 yards. The next 3.5 miles get easier until you are paddling flat water onto the lake behind Third Dam. Expect lots of overhanging bushes. Several other campgrounds through there offer other access points. There's about a mile of river between Third Dam and Second Dam.

LOGAN CANYON—SECOND DAM TO FIRST DAM

Difficulty: Class 3 to 4+.
Length: 1.6 miles.
Average Gradient: 150 ft./mi.
Season: May, June.
Time: 1 hour.
Character: Steep, rocky, fast, holes, log potential, low pipe.
Levels: >300 cfs.
Elevation: Put-in 4900 ft., take-out 4650 ft.
Topo Maps: Logan Peak, Logan.
Permits: No.
Shuttle Length: Same as run.
Access: From U.S. 89 in Logan Canyon.

You can put in for the last section of the canyon just below lower Second Dam, but you might have to get out above a footbridge a half mile down if the level is really high. It's easier to simply put in below the footbridge (just above milepost 376). Below it is a steep, slanting drop off a diversion dam. It's runnable on the right when the water level is right. Scout it first. From there down, you're in for a wild ride. It's constant Class 3 to 4+ for almost two miles with only tiny eddies for stopping. You may want to walk and scout the whole section before running, especially in really high water. The hardest section starts a little above where the road crosses the river on down to a little below the bridge. The lake behind First (State) Dam is a good take-out.

All parts of the Logan Canyon section should be run with care. A tree could easily fall across it and the numerous small trees and bushes that overhang the river can act as strainers.

CITY SECTION (First Dam to Main Street)

Difficulty: Class 2 to 3-.
Length: 3 miles.
Average Gradient: 50 ft./mi.
Season: May, June,
Time: 1 to 2 hours.
Character: Fast urban stream, brushy, bridges, diversion dams.
Levels: >250 cfs.
Elevation: Put-in 4640 ft., take-out 4520 ft.
Topo Maps: Logan.
Permits: No.
Shuttle Length: Same as run.
Access: U.S. 89 at the mouth of Logan Canyon, Main Street and 600 South. Canyon Road follows the river just below First Dam with several local streets off it, such as Crocket and Riverside Drive, going to access points.

This is a pretty run for an urban river. Some areas are lined with cottonwood trees that completely canopy the river. There are many beautiful homes. Overhanging bushes make stopping difficult in high water.

Shortly below First Dam is the "ender hole" with a reversal creating a great play spot. This has been used for rodeos. There is a fairly large diversion dam about a third of the way through this run. The river goes left off a cement drop. There's a footbridge right above it. Land in the canal and check the drop. It can be run at some levels. The "V Wave" is a drop under a bridge at 100 North and Riverside Drive. Another drop is in someone's backyard. At some levels there is a pretty good hole. If you decide not to run it, you'll have to hop out in their yard and get right back in. The river bank becomes more overgrown after this drop as you near Main Street.

The bank below Main is even more overgrown. The current continues swift until after the next road crossing. Beginners will enjoy the river after Mendon and on down to Cutler Reservoir.

MAMMOTH CREEK

Difficulty: Class 1 to 3-.
Length: 7 miles.
Average Gradient: 45 ft./mi.
Season: May, early June.
Time: 2 to 3 hours.
Character: Small, wooded, fences, continuous, much steeper sections upstream.
Levels: >250 cfs.
Elevation: Put-in 7840 ft., take-out 7515 ft.
Topo Maps: Brian Head, Panguitch Lake, Henrie Knolls, Asay Bench, Haycock Mountain.
Permits: No.
Shuttle Length: 8 miles.
Access: From I-15 and Cedar City, take Highway 14 east until you pass Navajo Lake. Look for a sign for Mammoth Creek about 6 miles past the lake. Go north on this paved road. The take-out is about 3 miles down the side road to Hatch. Stay on the paved road for the put-in where it crosses Mammoth Creek. There are a number of homes in this area. To get there from U.S. 89, go south of Hatch a little over a mile. Look for a road going to the fish hatchery. Do not turn off at the fork to the hatchery but continue up the canyon about 5 more miles until the road crosses Mammoth Creek. This is the take-out for the described run or put-in for the lower part. For the put-in, continue up the road. Turn right on the paved road and follow until you cross Mammoth Creek again. Steeper runs are available higher up.

This is one of the major tributaries to the Sevier River. I heard about this from a fisherman. There is a lot more potential for runs there. When Rob Burton and I checked it out recently, it was in flood stage with water into the bushes and trees and very swift water. Parts that we didn't run looked very boatable—provided there were no obstructions. The high water didn't leave any way to stop in most places and scouting was impossible due to private property. Much of the river is hidden, even though there are roads close by. We saw at least one fence across and some downed trees. At low flows more could be safely checked out from the river.

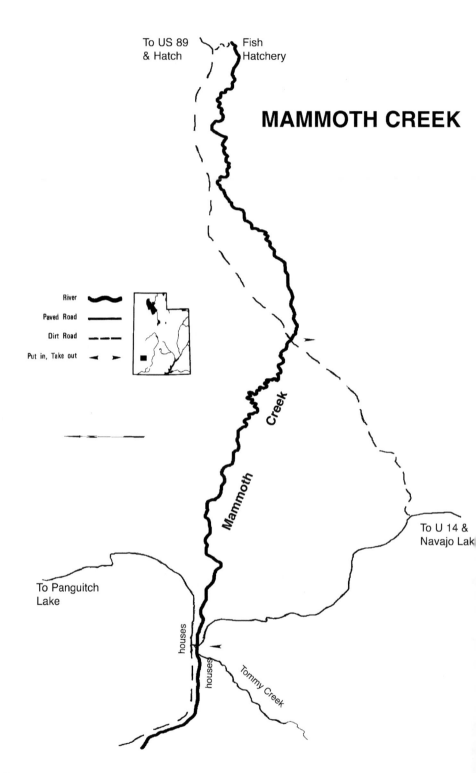

To US 89
& Hatch

Fish
Hatchery

MAMMOTH CREEK

River
Paved Road
Dirt Road
Put in, Take out

Creek

Mammoth

To U 14 &
Navajo Lak

To Panguitch
Lake

houses

houses

Tommy Creek

Almost all the surrounding land along its entire length is private, so access is limited.

There is a very beautiful section starting at the bridge just below where Tommy Creek joins. The river flows swiftly past a number of homes into a small wooded canyon. The river is mainly Class 2 with a couple of slightly harder spots. There were two barbed-wire fences. The canyon opens in about 3 miles into a large valley where the river covers 4 more miles meandering from one side of the valley to the other, splitting frequently, and making slow headway to the far end. There were two fences through this stretch.

The river picks up speed again after going under the road at the end of the valley. It looks like a potentially good run of about 8 miles out to U.S. 89. There is no access that we could find that wasn't private land until the fish hatchery just above U.S. 89. Immediately above the hatchery, the river was screaming through the bushes and trees. There was no way to scout this steep part due to private property. It was so fast and high, with no way to stop if there was a problem, that we didn't run it.

MUDDY CREEK

Difficulty: Class 1 to 3-.

Length: 47 miles from I-70 to Hidden Splendor mine.

Average Gradient: 22 ft./mi.

Season: May, June.

Time: 1 to 3 days.

Character: Small, rocky, remote, flash flood potential.

Levels: >80 cfs for The Chute, >120 for the rest.

Elevation: I-70 5640 ft., Hidden Splendor Mine 4640 ft.

Topo Maps: Flagstaff Peak, Emery West, Emery East, Mesa Butte, Big Bend Draw, Ireland Mesa, Tomsich Butte, Hunt Draw, Little Wild Horse Mesa, Skyline Rim, The Notch.

Permits: No.

Shuttle Length: I-70 and Muddy Creek to Tomsich Butte is 60 miles; Tomsich Butte to Hidden Splendor Mine is 15 miles.

Access: U-10 near Emery and dirt roads off it for upper sections, I-70 and dirt road to Reds Canyon and Tomsich Butte for The Chute, dirt road from there to Hidden Splendor Mine for take-out, or Factory Butte road (14 miles of dirt) off U-24 west of Hanksville to take out after going through the San Rafael Reef. The bridge north of Hanksville on U-24 if going all the way down Muddy Creek.

It's really too bad Muddy Creek rarely has water, because it's an incredible desert river. There is some paddling above highway 10. I've run only a couple miles of this, from a little above the "end of county maintenance" sign to the gauge and first diversion dam. This is Class 2 with a little Class 3-. Not far below the diversion dam is another dam. So there are two major diversion dams below the gauge. This is why you can get a reading of 200 cfs from the gauge on the internet or flow phone and go down to run The Chute and find it almost dry.

Another interesting stretch of Muddy Creek is from Highway 10 to Miller Canyon. The river cuts a surprisingly deep and narrow canyon through there. This 9-mile section takes about 3 to 4 hours to run. It's very winding at first. Watch out for fences. Then the river splits so many times that it's hard to find a main channel. You may have to walk a short distance before they come together. This will happen again in another half

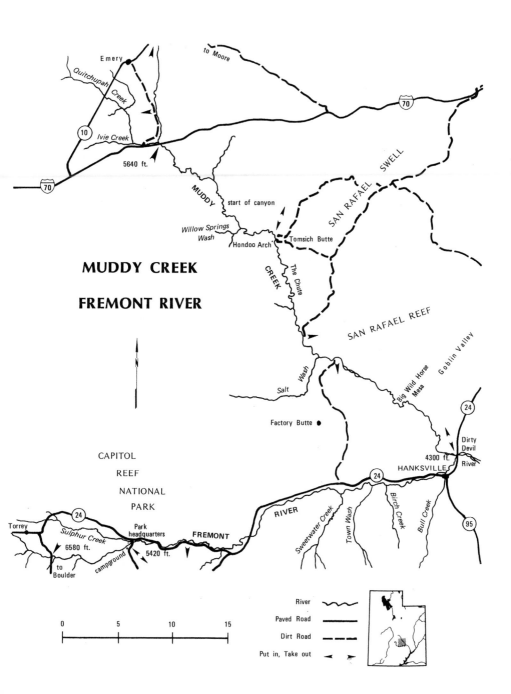

MUDDY CREEK

FREMONT RIVER

Muddy Creek. Photo by Ed Gertler.

mile. Once you get to the power lines, it will take 10 minutes to go under them because the river winds so much. Once you finally get to where the canyon narrows, the river is great. The scenery becomes spectacular, the river runs straighter, and there are a few boulders to dodge to liven things up. The bushes overhang the river. Since very few people go through there, spider webs stretch from one side to the other. I must have broken through hundreds of these. Let someone else go first.

You can continue paddling to I-70, but the only people I know who have done it said they wouldn't do it again. There are too many bushes and trees all the way across the river.

I-70 is a better place to start if there is enough water and you have a few days to paddle through the San Rafael Swell. I believe the old gauge downstream of the I-70 bridge is gone. You will just have to eyeball it or call the BLM office in Hanksville to see what the flow is there.

The river is swift, with many Class 1 to 3 rocky rapids that can be tricky for a canoe or raft. You may see cattle for a while. Lone Tree Crossing is about 11 miles down. A dirt road comes in there, making it a possible put-in. The river slows and you enter a narrower canyon as the river cuts into the Navajo Sandstone. Sand waves liven things up. It's about 15 miles from I-70 to Cat Canyon and 23 miles to Willow Springs Wash (Mussentuchit [Mustn't Touch It] Wash).

The river soon cuts into the Wingate Sandstone and you come to Tomsich Butte, almost 31 miles from I-70. A road comes in there to some old cabins and mines, offering another access point. Many people launch from this area to do a day run through The Chute.

Hondoo Arch is below on the right. The river picks up speed and cuts through the Moenkopi Formation, a deep reddish layer, into a harder, lighter colored, and smoother layer called Coconino Sandstone. A good rapid after a sharp right turn leads into a narrow canyon. This lasts about a half mile and then the cliff lowers until you go around a bend and pick it up again. This is The Chute. You're in a narrow, swift (Class 1) corridor of wall-to-wall water. In some places the cliffs are so high and overhanging that you can't see the sky. It is so narrow that in some places it's hard to turn a kayak sideways. Near the end of The Chute, the canyon narrows to about 7 feet wide at river level and is even narrower about 20 feet up where flash floods have left a logjam that you paddle under.

After you come out of this box canyon, the rapids are almost continuous for a couple of miles. After a particularly good rapid some partially hidden old buildings are encountered. This is the Hidden Splendor Mine area. A road comes in there, making this a possible take-out. It's about 11 miles to the end of The Chute and then 5 more to Hidden Splendor Mine.

If you continue, you will rise through all the rock layers you've dropped through since leaving I-70. These layers drop sharply as you cut through the San Rafael Reef. It's about 7 miles from the mine to the Factory Butte road, offering another chance to take out.

With enough water, you can continue through more open terrain for another 24 miles to the junction with the Fremont River and the bridge by Hanksville. This is the beginning of the Dirty Devil River.

This is fragile country. It takes a long time for plants you kill to grow back. Trash and waste don't decay in such a dry area. So take care. Leave things better than you found them.

≈ ≈ ≈ **OGDEN RIVER**

Map: See p. 19.

Difficulty: Class 1 to 3.
Length: 6.5 miles.
Average Gradient: 63 ft./mi.
Season: May, June.
Time: 2 to 3 hours.
Character: Small, even gradient, trees.
Levels: >200 cfs, best when gauge is above 3.0 ft.
Elevation: Put-in 5440 ft., take-out 5080 ft.
Topo Maps: Causey Dam, Browns Hole.
Permits: No.
Shuttle Length: Same as run.
Access: From Ogden, take Highway 39 up Ogden Canyon past Pineview
   Reservoir. In Huntsville turn right so you are continuing on Highway
   39. This will take you past the take-out and along the river. If going
   all the way to Causey Dam, watch for the sign and a turnoff to the
   right. Weber County Memorial Park is just below the dam and
   makes a good put-in. Since the road follows the river, you can get in
   or out just about anywhere you want.

This is a pleasant run with nice camping in the area. You can expect a few
trees across the river, so be alert. There is a small, usually runnable, diversion
dam that can be seen from the road. Just above the South Fork Campground, the river goes left to the hillside and there are some pipes on the
left. Just below is a cement structure with a little drop creating a good surf
wave at some levels. Bathrooms and water are available at the campgrounds.

The hardest rapid is not far above the take-out. It's where the road
makes an S-turn bend. The bottom part of the rapid can be seen from
the road. It's a good idea to scout this from the drive to decide if you
want to run it or not. A good take-out is from 10450 East, about a mile
below the hardest rapid, at a diversion dam. I don't know what the land
status is. It's mainly private below there.

Difficulty: Class 2 to 5.
Length: 5 miles in canyon, 2 to 3 miles in town.
Average Gradient: 80 ft./mi., 40 ft./mi.
Season: May, June, dam controlled.
Time: 1 to 4 hours.
Character: Steep, small, low bridges, possible logs, highway creates un-
   natural streambed.
Levels: >200 cfs.
Elevation: Put-in 4900 ft., take-out Washington Boulevard 4300 ft.
Topo Maps: Huntsville, North Ogden, Ogden.
Permits: No.
Shuttle Length: About the same as run.
Access: Highway 39 (12th Street in Odgen) follows the river or close to
   it. Harrison and Washington Boulevards cross it.

There is a good put-in below Pineview Reservoir from a dirt road just
above the water treatment plant. The first part is mainly Class 1 and 2
with a few slightly harder sections. You may have trouble fitting under a
footbridge at very high water (1000+ cfs). High water also makes it much
faster and pushier. The Alaskan Inn is passed partway through the run.
The river drops more steeply after that.

   The last two miles in the canyon are the hardest. Be sure to scout.
At flows of 300 to 500 cfs, this is mainly Class 3 and 4. It's Class 4+ at
flows above this, changing to 5- at flows above about 800 cfs. The hardest
part of high water is the lack of eddies. A swim can be long, with flush
drownings a real possibility. There are also occasional log problems.
There is a fairly permanent one just after going under the highway near
the mouth of the canyon. A kayaker died in this lower stretch a few years
ago.

   The river flows past a restaurant at the mouth of the canyon, goes
under a side road, and enters a parkway area that goes past Eccles Dinosaur Park. This section has a number of fun and easy man-made drops.
Access is good all along there. There is a good take-out at the park
below the dinosaur area. If you continue, overhanging bushes may block
the way, requiring a short portage.

The next road you go under is Harrison Boulevard. Below, at Gramercy (850 East) and Park Boulevard (about 1800 South), there is a great play wave under the bridge at flows above 300 cfs. It becomes superb at flows over 800 cfs. If you swim there, keep your feet up, as there are metal bars under the water. There is a short rocky drop not far downstream. The next major road is Washington Boulevard.

≈ ≈ ≈ PRICE RIVER

SCOFIELD RESERVOIR TO KYUNE

Difficulty: Class 1 to 2+.
Length: 15 miles.
Average Gradient: 40 ft./mi.
Season: May, June, dam controlled.
Time: 4 to 5 hours.
Character: Small, wooded, fairly steady gradient, log problems, fences.
Levels: >250 cfs.
Elevation: Put-in 7600 ft., take-out 7040 ft.
Topo Maps: Colton, Kyune
Permits: No.
Shuttle Length: 11.5 miles to U.S. 6, 3.5 more to Kyune.
Access: Take U.S. 6 from Price or Spanish Fork. Take the turnoff to Sco-
field Reservoir (U-96). Put in below the dam. For the take-out, go
2 miles farther south on U.S. 6 to where you cross the Price River
or continue another 3 miles and turn left at the Emma Park Road
(mile 221) and go to the bridge (the USGS map shows this as Kyune).

I'm not sure what's legal as far as putting in right below Scofield Reservoir. The first mile is fairly flat with logs possible all the way across. There
is an occasional small rapid. A railroad roughly follows the river. When
the tracks cross from the left to the right and the canyon narrows, there
are several good Class 2 rapids, with the best lying under the bridge as
the tracks cross back. After a footbridge come several more rapids.
Watch for a small white fence on the left coming from the tracks. There
may be a wire crossing the river. Another good rapid follows in a quarter
of a mile.

The best rapids for this section are in a mile-long stretch cutting
through a cottonwood grove. Watch out for logs. Just after entering this
wooded section, the railroad crosses again to the right. As the cottonwoods end, a barbed-wire fence crosses.

When the canyon opens, there is a steel cable hanging across the
river. You enter the last narrow canyon shortly after. This is the section
you see from U.S. 6. The river is fast and smooth until you come to a

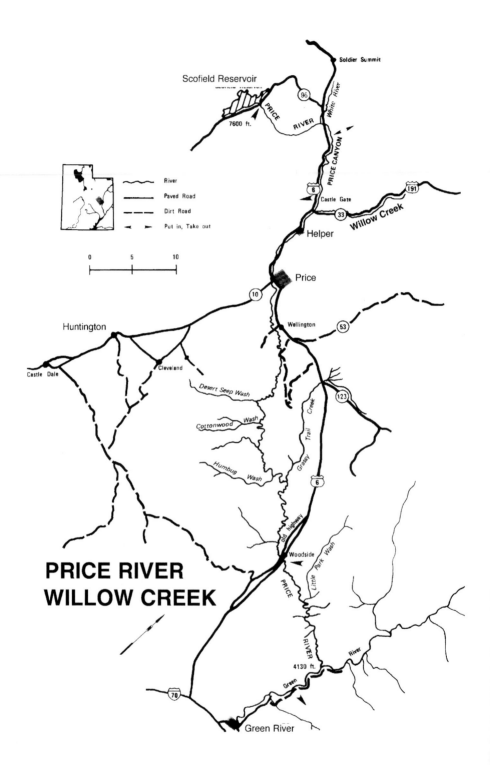

Scofield Reservoir

Soldier Summit

7600 ft.

96

PRICE RIVER

White River

PRICE CANYON

6

191

Castle Gate

33

Willow Creek

Helper

Price

10

Wellington

53

Huntington

Cleveland

Desert Seep Wash

123

Castle Dale

Cottonwood Wash

Grassy Trail Creek

Humbug Wash

6

Old highway

Woodside

Little Park Wash

**PRICE RIVER
WILLOW CREEK**

PRICE RIVER

River

4130 ft.

Green

70

Green River

River

Paved Road

Dirt Road

Put in, Take out

0   5   10

Price River. Photo by Kirk Nichols.

couple of small rapids under U.S. 6. Another 4 miles of easy meandering river get you to the take-out. Get out above the bridge and climb the short steep bank to the road. Continue only if you are prepared for harder whitewater.

Price Canyon

Difficulty: Class 3 to 4+.
Length: 8 miles to mile marker 228.
Average Gradient: 90 ft./mi.
Season: May, June, dam controlled.
Time: 3 hours.
Character: Steep, rocky, narrow, continuous, unnatural riverbed, log problems.
Levels: >250 cfs, not on phone or Internet sites.
Elevation: Put-in 7040 ft., take-out 6300 ft.
Topo Maps: Kyune, Standardville, Helper.

Permits: No.

Shuttle Length: About the same as run.

Access: U.S. 6 follows it. At the top of the canyon, take the Emma Park Road (mile 221) and put in where the road crosses the river (the USGS map shows this as Kyune). Since the road follows the river, there are many access points.

Much of this section is steep, continuous, and rocky. At high water (which is extremely rare), it can be very pushy, with few eddies for stopping. Generally, you're lucky to have enough water to run at all. Lower flows are much easier—Class 2 to 3+. The riverbed is mostly unnatural due to a highway on one side and a railroad on the other, so expect sharp rock, cement, and metal in places.

There is an old picnic area off a side road (Emma Park Road) at the top of Price Canyon. The side road crosses the Price River and makes a good put-in. The rapids start right around the first bend. If this is too hard, get out, because it will get much harder. The river does calm down temporarily after this first section. The railroad crosses the river and goes through a tunnel, giving you a short section of "natural" river, without highway or railroad. In about three-quarters of a mile, the railroad crosses the river again. The river soon makes a big loop away from the road for almost 1.5 miles, but the railroad still follows. The river eases up partway through this until you get back to the road.

The rapids are pretty continuous from there on, with the difficulty increasing as you go. The hardest rapid is just above milepost 226. At low water, it is very rocky. At high water, it can be hard to stop. There were two of us the first time we ran it. We were going to stop in a tiny eddy at the brink of the drop and scout it. I made it into the eddy but my friend had a hard time catching it with me already there. He didn't quite make it and ended up running the rapid backward. I chased him and we both ended up doing fine. So you may want to stop higher up or scout from the road. There's some vertical pin potential there, especially in a small low-volume boat.

Two more miles of exciting paddling take you to a good take-out a little before milepost 228. The bank isn't as steep there. The turnout by an old boarded-up mine is a good place to leave a car.

If you continue on to Helper, add another 5 miles to the mileage listed above and plan on a few portages. Shortly below the mile 228 take-out, there is a small runnable drop and then a diversion dam to portage. There is a big drop right at the narrow spot in the canyon called Castle Gate. This is full of junk and requires a short portage. It can be seen from the road and is just above the water treatment plant. You will go under a bridge as the river cuts left. After the river turns right, a small shack is visible on the left at another diversion dam that is behind the water tank. Scout and decide if you want to run it.

For the next 2 miles, there are no more dams, but there is one low footbridge that may require some serious ducking. The next diversion dam is broken and has a slot in the middle that is usually runnable. The next dam is very dangerous. It's a double drop immediately after a bridge. This can be seen from the highway. Fortunately, the water is slow right above it, making it easy to stop and portage. Do not blunder into it. You most likely would not survive. A fast rapid section leads to another drop. This looks runnable from the road but is full of sharp metal rails. Not far below is another unrunnable drop of about 8 feet. The steep banks make the portage difficult. There is a good take-out bridge a little farther, in Helper. It's about 5 more miles to the dam at the golf course where the river is almost totally diverted during the summer. I've never run this part.

WELLINGTON TO WOODSIDE

Topo Maps: Wellington, Olsen Reservoir, Mounds, Flat Top Mountain, Grassy, Woodside.

This is a long, seldom run section. I have never run this stretch. The description here is from a friend who ran it. He put in at Wellington. Within a mile there is a 5-foot dam to be portaged. Three bridges side by side are the next landmarks, one for the railroad and two for roads. About 3 miles from the put-in, near a coal preparation plant, is a footbridge with a 2-foot dam beneath. Just around two short bends is a 10-foot unrunnable dam.

The river is mostly smooth and winding in the upper part, with visibility hindered by high banks and bushes. This improves as you go. A road crosses the river about 64 miles above the mouth. The canyon that gradually forms continues until several miles below Grassy Trail Creek. The rapids are frequent, sometimes long above this creek and Class 1, becoming Class 2 below it. The canyon opens to views of the Book Cliffs.

Difficulty: Class 2 to 3. One Class 4
Length: 24 miles.
Average Gradient: 25 ft./mi.
Season: May, June.
Time: 6 to 8 hours.
Character: Remote desert canyon, rocky, minor log problems.
Levels: >300 cfs, the higher the better.
Elevation: Put-in 4600 ft., take-out 4140 ft.
Topo Maps: Woodside, Cliff, Jenny Canyon, Butler Canyon.
Permits: No.
Shuttle Length: About 38 miles if you get out at Swasey Rapid.
Access: Launch from U.S. 6 at Woodside or down a dirt road from there
   on the north side of the river. Take out by continuing on U.S. 6 to
   I-70 and going east to the town of Green River. Go through town to
   the east side of the river and take Hastings Road to the BLM take-
   out or go another quarter mile to Swasey Rapid and beach. There is
   camping available.

Woodside consists of a gas station and some old buildings. It used to be
a tourist area where a geyser was the big attraction when the old highway was in use. The geyser can still be seen in the distance when it occasionally goes off. The owner of the gas station is friendly and very familiar
with the area. Stop in for gas and information. He owns the land in the
area, including where a lot of people put in. Ask his permission before
launching, or take a dirt road from the east side of the highway that follows the north side of the river. He may also be able to help you with a
shuttle for a reasonable fee.

There is a gauge where the old highway crosses the Price River. To
get to it you will have to get permission to cross the private land at
Woodside or go up the road about a mile to where there is a connecting
road. The minimum that I'd be willing to run this is about 4 feet. I'm sure
it could be run lower. It is much better to run it above 5.5 feet.

The river is flat and very winding for about 6 miles as you make
your way to where the canyon starts. This can be avoided by taking the
dirt road (ugly when really wet) just north and across from the gas station. Follow it to where it crosses the river. Most of the rapids start

below this point. Most of the rapids are not big but they are fairly frequent and do require a fair amount of maneuvering to avoid hitting rocks. One new Class 4 has been added about three-fourths of the way through. There is an interesting old cabin and corral about a mile before you get to the Green River.

Depending on water level and where you put in, it can take a full day to get to the Green River. From there you can paddle for another hour or two to Swasey Beach to get out or take out wherever you can on the dirt road that follows the Green River. (See Green River, Gray Canyon section.)

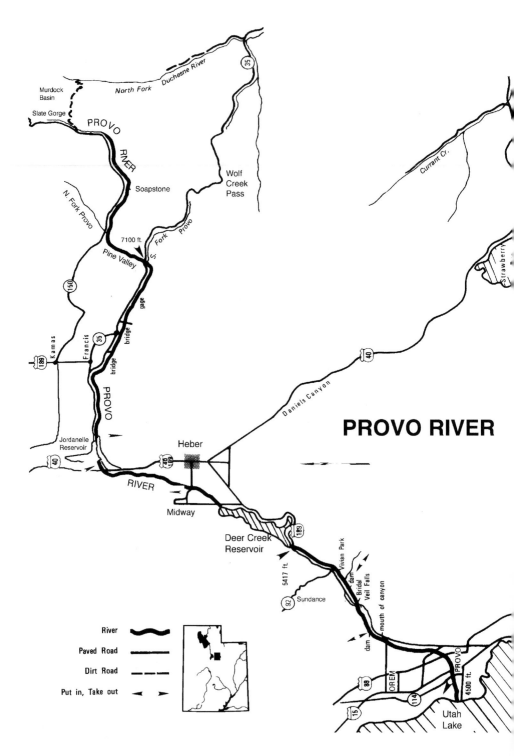

Murdock Basin

Slate Gorge

North Fork Duchesne River

35

PROVO RIVER

Wolf Creek Pass

Soapstone

N. Fork Provo

7100 ft.

S. Fork Provo

Pine Valley

gage

150

bridge

bridge

Kamas

Francis

35

189

Currant Cr.

Strawberry

40

Daniels Canyon

PROVO

Jordanelle Reservoir

Heber

PROVO RIVER

40

40 189

RIVER

Midway

Deer Creek Reservoir

189

Vivian Park

5417 ft.

dam

Bridal Veil Falls

mouth of canyon

92

Sundance

River	~~~~~
Paved Road	———
Dirt Road	– – –
Put in, Take out	◄ — ►

dam

89

OREM

114

PROVO

4500 ft.

15

Utah Lake

≈ ≈ ≈ PROVO RIVER

PROVO RIVER FALLS TO SOAPSTONE

Difficulty: Class 4 to 5.
Length: 1 to 10 miles.
Average Gradient: 150 ft./mi., much greater at times.
Season: Late May, June, early July.
Time: 1 hour to all day.
Character: Steep and continuous mountain stream, falls, logs, channel
     splitting, beautiful scenery.
Levels: >100 cfs.
Elevation: Put-in 9400 ft., take-out 7760 ft.
Topo Maps: Mirror Lake, Soapstone Basin.
Permits: No.
Shuttle Length: Same as run.
Access: Highway 150 out of Kamas follows it.

Provo River Falls is a series of 5 falls with very little break between them,
with drops of 10 to 20 feet each. The landings are shallow. They were
first run by Mark White. I know of only one other group that has run
them since. This is the steepest runnable section of river that I know of
in Utah. The river is fast and steep on down to where it goes under
Highway 150, a possible access point.

   The river soon enters Slate Gorge, where you will encounter 3
major waterfalls and several smaller ones. The first is almost always full of
trees and, if so, unrunnable. Check carefully before running these falls. The
second and third are double drops, with the second being the most runnable. Once past the big waterfalls, the paddling is easier but still steep,
tight, and fast. It can be hard to stop above a tree that might block the
river, so scout carefully. The gorge opens and there's about a mile of easier paddling to a good take-out at the bridge for the Murdock Basin Road.

   The river stays a little easier for about a mile until you come to a
stretch of smooth, sloping ledges that plunge the river into another
gorge. This, again, needs to be thoroughly scouted for logs. I have never
found this section free of trees, and they always seem to be in bad places
for stopping. There aren't any big falls but there are a couple of smaller

Upper Provo River.

ones that are fun to run if they are clean. As the gorge opens, there is a possible take-out on the right where a dirt road comes in, or continue a short distance farther to Cobblerest Campground.

About a mile below Cobblerest Campground, water from the Duchesne Tunnel comes in, increasing the flow substantially at times. There is a fast quarter-mile section below this, and then expect to walk as much as you paddle. High water would be scary through here. There always seems to be logjam after logjam, as the river splits into many channels. Things get slightly better around Soapstone Campground and down to the Soapstone Road.

SOAPSTONE ROAD TO JORDANELLE RESERVOIR

Difficulty: Class 2 to 3.
Length: 23 miles.
Average Gradient: 75 ft./mi.
Season: Late May, June, early July.
Time: 1 hour to 1 long day.
Character: Fairly steep, continuous, rocky, wooded, logs, fences, bridges.
Levels: >300 cfs, lower parts near Woodland need >500 cfs but >800 cfs is best.
Elevation: Put-in 7760 ft., take-out 6040 ft.
Topo Maps: Soapstone, Woodland, Francis, Heber City.
Permits: No.
Shuttle Length: Most parts are the same as run. If you go from the upper to the lower, you will need to drive roughly an extra 20 miles.
Access: Highway 150 follows down to Pine Valley. To get to the lower half, follow U-150 down to Kamas. Go south on U.S. 189 to Francis and take U-35 to the Woodland area. This accesses the lower end of Pine Valley. U.S. 189 follows the river to Jordanelle Reservoir.

From Soapstone, along Highway 150 until the North Fork comes in, the river is mainly Class 2 with an occasional log problem. The worst of the logs is usually in the upper part of this. As the river swings away from the highway and heads into Pine Valley, the logs get bad again. The river splits and both parts have lots of trees across. The rapids are generally easy. The land is private.

The river is more enjoyable once you go under U-35, the road going up the South Fork. The river stays more in one channel, with fewer trees, and more playing and excitement. There are many cabins and homes through there. About 2 miles down is a gauge where the river goes next to the road. 3.0 feet is a good medium level of about 800 cfs.

The river swings left away from the road. About halfway to the Woodland bridge is a diversion dam. Its slanting, rocky drop can be run in a few spots at the right water level. Scout first. A little farther, what looks like a broken diversion dam is usually runnable. The river splits up more until the bridge from Woodland. It's just over 6 miles from the U-35 bridge to the Woodland bridge. Turn by the church in Woodland to get to this bridge.

It's about 9 more miles to Jordanelle Reservoir. It takes about a half hour to get to the next bridge at 1000 East. Most of the land is private. The river is fairly fast and splits into channels at times. The area is quite beautiful and wooded. Watch out for fences and trees. Get out above the state park at Jordanelle to avoid paying a fee.

JORDANELLE RESERVOIR TO DEER CREEK RESERVOIR

This 8-mile section is in the process of changing. It has been heavily channelized with a series of drops to slow the water. Some of the drops are also diversion dams. The meanders are being put back in. This will slow the river, lengthen it, eliminate some drops, and create better fishing. It will actually increase the length by about 2 miles. The only bad thing is that we lose the excitement of faster water and running the 7 drops that were there. It should make it a beautiful run for beginners. The changes aren't all made, so I don't know exactly what this will be like. There will probably still be diversion dams and possible tree hazards, but the slower gradient should make it easier to deal with these. This area can be accessed from the side road off U.S. 40 going to the Jordanelle Dam and the road going to Midway.

DEER CREEK RESERVOIR TO Upper DIVERSION DAM

Difficulty: Class 1 to 2-.
Length: 6 miles.
Average Gradient: 15 ft./mi.

Season: All year, dam controlled.

Time: 2 to 3 hours.

Character: Fairly easy but fast in spots, a few rocks, wooded with rare log problems, bridge trestles in river.

Levels: >200 cfs.

Elevation: Put-in 5240 ft., take-out 5160 ft.

Topo Maps: Aspen Grove, Bridal Veil Falls.

Permits: No.

Shuttle Length: Roughly the same as river.

Access: U.S. 189 follows it.

This is a beautiful and fairly easy section. It is also excellent fishing, so you will be competing with all the fishermen. Some of them get upset when you go by no matter how hard you try to stay out of their way. There are no real rapids, but the water is swift, with some riffles in spots, and cold.

Dirt roads go down to the river just below the dam, offering several put-in possibilities. Watch out for a bridge about a quarter mile below the dam. The pillars go into the water and have destroyed several canoes that have wrapped around them. A little farther down, the river splits almost equally. The right channel goes past a privately owned campground and has a small footbridge across it. The left channel has also had a low bridge at times. At really high water you may not fit under these. The right channel is usually safer.

The biggest hazard on this stretch is where the railroad tracks cross the river with trestles in the water. This is about 2.5 river miles below the dam. Look for it on the drive and make sure you can recognize it. Coming down the river, you won't see it until the last minute due to a bend in the river. Many canoes have been destroyed there, with some people barely escaping with their lives. It's usually safer to run between trestles on the right, but the current throws you left. Left is sometimes plugged with trees. If you are not an experienced paddler, you may want to land above and walk your boat through.

There is some fast water below the bridge, with a stretch that has man-made rock outcroppings sticking out from the sides, creating some eddies and waves that are fun for a paddler but also good for fish. So this is one of the most heavily fished areas. The river runs swiftly past the turnoff to Sundance and the Alpine Loop. Below there are usually the most trees in the river.

The last part of the run, below Vivian Park (South Fork of Provo), is much slower. A side road to the diversion dam offers access to the river.

UPPER DIVERSION DAM TO THE MURDOCK (LOWER) DIVERSION DAM

Difficulty: Class 2 to 4.
Length: 4 miles.
Average Gradient: 70 ft./mi.
Season: May, June, dam controlled.
Time: 1 to 2 hours.
Character: Fast, rocky, wooded, so some log problems.
Levels: >250 cfs; really high flows can be challenging at Bridal Veil Falls.
Elevation: Put-in 5160 ft., take-out 4900 ft.
Topo Maps: Bridal Veil Falls, Orem.
Permits: No.
Shuttle Length: Same as run, jogging and bike path along it.
Access: U.S. 189 follows it.

The river looks calm below the diversion dam. This has lured unsuspecting beginners to put in—unaware that at the first bend the river suddenly narrows and drops through a rocky stretch. This is an intermediate to advanced stretch with channel splits, sharp turns, and often trees across or partially across. Soon after is Upper Falls Park. There are some excellent play waves in this area.

Class 2 rapids continue down to Bridal Veil Falls. The hardest stretch in this section then begins. At high water this is Class 4. The hardest part continues for several hundred yards until you are past an island that can hide trees across the river. Scout this stretch. Continuous Class 2 and 3 rapids take you under the highway and past Nunns Park. A parkway trail offers constant access to the river. You will pass through Canyon Glenn Park, where there is a steeper section that drops under the parkway trail. Across from the Squaw Flat road are several short drops where the river was altered a few years ago. The current dies as you reach the small lake behind the Murdock Diversion Dam. There is limited parking there.

Difficulty: Class 1 to 3 (P).
Length: Up to 9 miles.
Average Gradient: 40 ft./mi.
Season: May, June, dam controlled.
Time: 1 to 5 hours.
Character: Fast urban stretch, bridges, fences, dams, several play spots.
Levels: >200 cfs.
Elevation: Put-in 4900 ft., take-out Utah Lake 4500 ft.
Topo Maps: Orem, Provo.
Permits: No.
Shuttle Length: Varies, but about the same length as run.
Access: U.S. 189 follows the top part. There is also access from University Avenue, Orem's 800 North and Center Streets, University Parkway, U-114, State Park at Utah Lake.

During much of the summer this stretch is almost dry, most of the water being taken out at the diversion dam. This section primarily goes through the cities of Orem and Provo, past some very large and fancy homes. The river is mainly Class 2 while still in the canyon, becoming mostly Class 1 upon reaching the valley. There is fairly good current all the way until just before Utah Lake. Trees occasionally block the river, but the biggest and most dangerous obstacles are the five diversion dams. Some can be run and some can't.

The first two dams are close together by the mouth of the canyon at the power plant, just before you come to Orem's 800 North Street. They can both be run at the right level and in the right spot. Check them out and decide for yourself. The third dam is about a quarter mile past 800 North. Scout this before running. The fourth dam, just above a bridge about a block north of University Parkway, should be portaged. There's a park and picnic pavilion just above on the right. The fifth dam, immediately below a bridge where Columbia Lane crosses on Provo's west side, is a bad one, so portage. A good take-out is where the U-114 bridge crosses, or you can continue on to the state park at Utah Lake.

≈ ≈ ≈ ROCK CREEK

Map: See p. 102.
Difficulty: Class 3 to 4+.
Length: 5 miles.
Average Gradient: 100 ft./mi.
Season: Late May, June.
Time: 2 to 3 hours.
Character: Steep, rocky, logs, beautiful mountain stream.
Levels: >300 cfs; 3.7 on gauge at take-out bridge is ideal (about 600 cfs).
Elevation: Put-in 7980 ft., take-out 7480 ft.
Topo Maps: Tworoose Pass (the Upper Stillwater Reservoir is on the
    new version), Kidney Lake, Dry Mountain.
Permits: No.
Shuttle Length: Same as run.
Access: From U.S. 40 and Duchesne take Highway 87 north to Mountain
    Home and then take the road west and north to Rock Creek and
    the Upper Stillwater Reservoir.

Fortunately, the Central Utah Project didn't quite ruin this river. It isn't runnable as often as before, but in high-water years it can still be run. Rock
Creek has some of the more challenging rapids in the Uinta Mountains. The
first, Class 4+, is quite long; the second is only slightly easier.

Not far below the Upper Stillwater dam, the river picks up speed and
you enter a Class 3 rapid that swings to the left. The river then makes a
sharp right and slams into the undercut cliff on the left. Unless the river is
low, you can't tell it's undercut. The hardest rapid starts immediately after
this. Large boulders create steep drops and sharp turns.

You get a short break before the next hardest rapid. It's not as long
or as steep and the boulders are smaller, but there are more of them. Two
more rocky drops in the Class 3 to 3+ range are encountered in the next
quarter mile, then comes an easier section of Class 2 and 3 for about a
mile. Watch out for logs, especially when the river splits into smaller channels. When the channels come together, expect several Class 3 rapids. The
river then splits again but not as much. Take out at the bridge.

Much more of the river could be run but most of it is on the Indian
reservation and would require special permission.

≈ ≈ ≈ **SALINA CREEK**

Difficulty: Class 3 to 5.
Length: Up to 16 miles.
Average Gradient: 85 ft./mi.
Season: May, early June.
Time: 1 to 6 hours.
Character: Steep, rocky, fairly continuous, bridges, tunnels, some log
   problems.
Levels: >250 cfs.
Elevation: Put-in 6700 ft., take-out 5450 ft.
Topo Maps: Water Hollow Ridge, Steves Mountain, Salina.
Permits: No.
Shuttle Length: About the same as run.
Access: I-70 follows the river east of Salina. Exits and frontage road give
   access.

There is challenging paddling on Salina Creek when it is up. You can put
in from I-70 exit 72. A frontage road takes you back downstream to
where the canyon narrows and the river steepens. The river is Class 2 at
first and then there is almost a mile of steeper Class 3 and 4 whitewater
with some big boulders. This could be Class 5 at really high water.

One of the unique things about this river is running through tunnels
under the freeway. First make sure they are clear. Also, make sure you
know where the obstacles are at the lower end. You accelerate through
the tunnel and then hit into a curling wave as you reach the slower
water. This blinds you at a time you may have to make a critical move.

After the second freeway tunnel, the river has a steep drop followed
shortly by another drop as it is squeezed by the cliff and road. This is behind where the frontage road goes through a tunnel.

There is a double freeway tunnel by Water Hollow. You'll find a good
rapid at Maple Spring Canyon where the river is pinched between a cliff
and the frontage road. In a little less than a mile the frontage road
crosses the river and climbs away from it. The river then cuts away from
the freeway for a short ways and then cuts back under it. The river then
gets easier and goes back under the freeway by Cottonwood Canyon.

At the Gooseberry road, you will find three square tunnels. The first

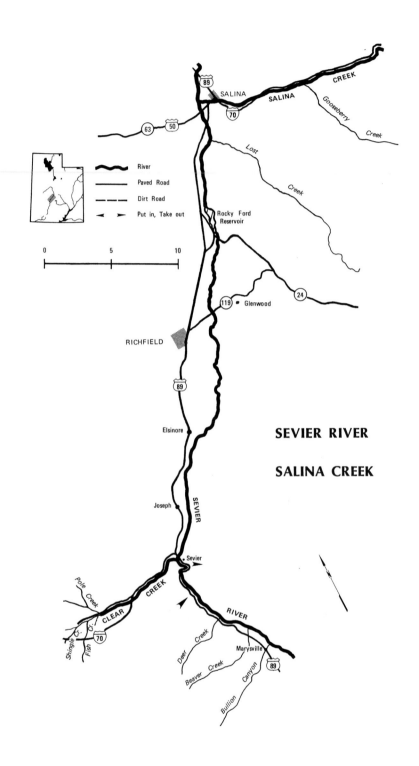

River
Paved Road
Dirt Road
Put in, Take out

0   5   10

SALINA

89

70

63   50

CREEK

SALINA

Gooseberry

Creek

Lost

Creek

Rocky Ford
Reservoir

119   Glenwood

24

RICHFIELD

89

Elsinore

SEVIER RIVER

SALINA CREEK

Joseph

SEVIER

Sevier

Pole

Creek

CLEAR   CREEK

70

Shingle Cr.

Fish Cr.

Deer   Creek

Marysville

Beaver   Creek

Bullion   Canyon

RIVER

89

Salina Creek.

is right above the road, the second under the road, the third just below. Gooseberry Creek enters a half mile farther. This begins a long Class 2 to 3 section that becomes entrenched in sheer dirt banks. About 3 miles below the Gooseberry road is a Class 6 entrance to a Class 4+ to 5-rapid. This is Pinball Rapid. Don't blunder into it. The entrance is usually unrunnable due to logs. The rest is steep, fast, rocky, and continually changing as the banks erode. This can be scouted from the frontage road. It is probably best to get out shortly after this rapid. The best whitewater is over and you will have to deal with a couple diversion dams if you continue.

≈ ≈ ≈ SAN JUAN RIVER

Baars and Stevenson's "San Juan Canyons" is an excellent map of the river.

Difficulty: Class 1 to 3.
Length: Up to 84 miles.
Average Gradient: 8 ft./mi.
Season: April-October.
Time: 1 to 6 days.
Character: Remote desert river, faster than most big desert rivers, historical sites, petroglyphs, ruins.
Levels: >450 cfs; bigger rafts will need 800 cfs.
Elevation: Put-in 4800 ft., take-out 3700 ft.
Topo Maps: Bluff, White Rock Point, San Juan Hill, Mexican Hat, The Goosenecks, Goulding NE, Slickhorn Canyon East, Slickhorn Canyon West, Whirlwind Draw, Mikes Mesa.
Permits: Yes: BLM, San Juan Field Office, (435) 587-1544, http://www. blm.gov/ut/st/en/fo/monticello/recreation/san_juan_river.html.
Shuttle Length: 27 miles from Sand Island to Mexican Hat, 57 miles from Mexican Hat to Clay Hills Crossing, 84 miles from Sand Island to Clay Hills Crossing.
Access: Sand Island is about 3 miles west of the town of Bluff on U.S. 163 and then a side road to the river. There are two access points by Mexican Hat. One is immediately above the bridge. The main one is about a half mile east off U.S. 163 at a BLM launch site. To get to the take-out at Clay Hills, go north from Bluff on U.S. 191 or north from Mexican Hat on U-261, to U-95. Go west on U-95 to U-276. Follow this southwest for about 19 miles and take the 11-mile dirt road south to Clay Hills Crossing.

There is a flat-water section from Montezuma Creek to Bluff that is about 18 miles long. The south side of the river is Navajo Indian Reservation. Any hiking or camping on that side requires a permit from the reservation.

The most common sections to run are the 27 miles from Sand Island to Mexican Hat and the 57 miles from Mexican Hat to Clay Hills Crossing or combining both into one trip. Permits are required with a

SAN JUAN RIVER

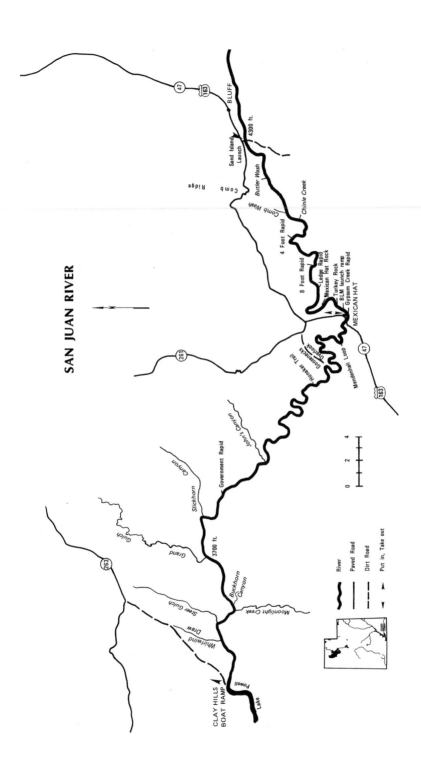

BLUFF

47
163

Sand Island Launch
4300 ft.

Butler Wash

Comb Ridge

Comb Wash

Chinle Creek

4 Foot Rapid

8 Foot Rapid

Ledge Rapid
Mexican Hat Rock
Turkey Rock
BLM launch ramp
Gypsum Creek Rapid

MEXICAN HAT

261

Honaker Trail

Goosenecks
Overlook

Mendenhall Loop

47

163

John's Canyon

Government Rapid

Slickhorn Canyon

Grand Gulch

263

3700 ft.

Buckhorn Canyon

Steer Gulch

Whirlwind Draw

Moonlight Creek

CLAY HILLS
BOAT RAMP

Powell Lake

River
Paved Road
Dirt Road
Put in, Take out

0   2   4

≈ 139

Goosenecks of the San Juan River.

fee that varies depending on which section you run. The fee season is from March 1 through October 31. Off-season trips still require a permit but no fee. Again, the south side of the river is off limits unless you have a permit from the Navajo Indians.

You will come to Butler Wash about 4 miles below Sand Island. There is some interesting hiking there. About a quarter mile below, on the right, are some petroglyphs. The best cliff dwelling is on the right just past mile 6, just before the cliff opens for Comb Wash. It's hard to see from the river. You will have to walk a few hundred yards to get to it.

The first 9 miles are in a wide canyon with green vegetation contrasting with the pink and reddish cliffs. The narrow canyon begins at about mile 9.5. Campsites can be hard to find. Look for them at wider spots where side canyons come in.

The waves and small rapids become quite frequent. There are several named rapids, with Eight Foot Rapid at mile 17 being the biggest for this section. The deep canyon ends just past mile 20. In another 3 miles, you pass Mexican Hat Rock overlooking the river on the right. Three more miles take you to a campground and river access point east of the small town of Mexican Hat. Around the corner is an island that splits Gypsum Creek Rapid. Your last access for the next 58 miles is just above the bridge at a short ramp leading up to Mexican Hat. This is also your last chance to stock up on cold drinks and ice. You will probably have to pay to get more water.

There are fewer riffles and rapids until you are through The Goosenecks. You come to Mendenhall Loop at mile 30. A short hike to the saddle takes you to an old cabin built by Walter E. Mendenhall, a gold prospector in the 1890s. On the far side of the loop, below the saddle, is the campsite register for Slickhorn Canyon and Grand Gulch.

At mile 37 you enter the famous Goosenecks. These huge meanders cover a lot of river miles for very few direct miles. At about miles 38.5 and 41, the Gooseneck Overlook is visible high on the cliff top to the north.

The Honaker Trail is on the right just after mile 44 and after a right bend in the river. There are several campsites in the area. The hike is well worthwhile, with incredible views. You will climb over 1200 feet in 2.5 miles. When you first look at the cliffs, it's hard to believe a trail could go up them. Gold fever drove people to amazing feats.

Many rapids are encountered between the Honaker Trail and Slickhorn Gulch. Government Rapid at mile 63.5 is the hardest. The rapid was made a little more challenging about two years ago. It's worth a scout, especially if you haven't been there for a while. Slickhorn Rapid can also be challenging at higher water levels.

Slickhorn Canyon, on the right at mile 66.3, has a number of campsites that should have been signed up for back at Mendenhall Loop. A hike up the canyon takes you to several nice pools.

Grand Gulch comes in on the right at mile 70. Permits are required for hiking more than 3 miles from the river. When Lake Powell is full, it backs up to about Grand Gulch and drowns the river's current. If the lake is low, you may have current all the way to Clay Hills Crossing. Watch out for shallow sand bars.

Do not go beyond Clay Hills Crossing. When Lake Powell is low, there is a waterfall about 2 miles below. The silt settling out of the river as it hit the reservoir created this. The silt then shifted the river at low lake levels over to a huge ledge where it pours off in a waterfall. This could disappear if the river ever shifts back.

≈ ≈ ≈ SAN RAFAEL RIVER

Map: See p. 42.

Map: See p. 42.

LITTLE GRAND CANYON

Difficulty: Class 1.
Length: 17 miles.
Average Gradient: 10 ft./mi.
Season: May, June.
Time: 1 to 2 days.
Character: Fairly gentle river through deep beautiful desert canyon.
Levels: >150 cfs unless you like walking your boat.
Elevation: Put-in 5260 ft., take-out 5100 ft.
Topo Maps: Sids Mountain, Bottleneck Peak.
Permits: No.
Shuttle Length: 18 miles.
Access: Take Highway 10 south from Price to about a mile north of
    Castle Dale. Turn off to the left on a dirt road going to Buckhorn
    Wash and The Wedge. Go about 13 miles and take the Wedge Over-
    look turnoff to the right and almost immediately take the road to
    the right going to Fuller Bottom. Go about 5.5 miles to the river. To
    get to the take-out, go back to the main dirt road, go right, and go
    down Buckhorn Wash. You will pass an excellent set of petroglyphs.
    Continue on until you cross the San Rafael River. The take-out is on
    the right and a BLM campground is on the left. You can also get to
    this area on a dirt road from I-70 and the Sinbad interchange.

The San Rafael River forms when three streams, Ferron Creek, Cottonwood Creek, and Huntington Creek, come together after draining the
10,000-foot peaks of the Wasatch Plateau. With enough water and a will-
ingness to paddle miles of slow meandering water, you could put in on
any of these tributaries where they go under Highway 10. Most people
put in at Fuller Bottom, off the road to The Wedge. This gets you close to
where the canyon starts.

　　The river flows swiftly through open desert country until it enters
an incredibly beautiful canyon cutting into the San Rafael Swell, a huge

Little Grand Canyon of the San Rafael River.

uplift that has been carved into massive buttes and deep serpentine canyons. The San Rafael River cuts one of the most majestic of these canyons. Unfortunately, it has a fairly short season.

There are no real rapids through this first canyon, just swift water, riffles, and a few sand waves. It's very beautiful, though, with sheer walls overhanging the river in spots. Several side canyons offer interesting hiking. Petroglyphs can be found in the area. Campsites are plentiful, or you can run it in a day. The canyon ends as it opens into a land of giant mesas and spires. Take out at the bridge by the San Rafael Campground.

BLACK BOXES

Difficulty: Class 3 to 4+ (P).
Length: 41 miles.
Average Gradient: 38 ft./mi.
Season: May, June.
Time: 1 to 2 days.
Character: Deep, sheer-walled gorges, pool/drop, boulders, chance of logs.

Levels: >200 cfs but under 1000 cfs.

Elevation: Put-in 5100 ft., take-out 4240 ft.

Topo Maps: Bottleneck Peak, Devils Hole, Drowned Hole Draw, Mexican Mountain, Spotted Wolf Canyon.

Permits: No.

Shuttle Length: 11.5 miles for upper box, 38 miles for both boxes, 50 miles for lower box.

Access: Take Highway 10 south from Price to about a mile north of Castle Dale. Turn off to the left on a dirt road going to Buckhorn Wash. Go past The Wedge and down Buckhorn Wash. You will pass a nice set of petroglyphs. Continue on until you get to the San Rafael River. Go southeast on the side road on the east side of the river for other access points or for the take-out of the upper box or to run just the lower box. To get to the take-out for the lower box, cross the San Rafael River on the main dirt road and continue for about 19 miles to I-70. Go east on I-70 to the Hanksville exit. Get back on I-70 going the other direction until you cross back over the San Rafael River. Go about three-quarters of a mile farther and take a dirt road heading north (go through a gate). Follow the dirt road for 1.8 miles (past Black Dragon Wash) to the end of the road. Make sure you can identify this spot when coming down the river.

The Upper and Lower Black Boxes are where the action is on the San Rafael River. Once you enter these box canyons, you are quite committed. There is almost nowhere to get out without climbing gear. They become quite dangerous above 1000 cfs. I know of two parties in different years that attempted the run at higher flows. They both ended up leaving their kayaks in the Upper Black Box and climbing out and waiting for a week for the river to drop. Both boxes can be run in one long day, or they make a great two-day trip.

If you don't mind a few extra miles of flatwater, you can put in at the bridge by the BLM campground. A side road roughly parallels the river on the northeast side. You can put in off this in a couple different places and save a few miles of paddling. The run is 22 miles from the bridge to the old Mexican Mountain Road, with smooth water for almost 10 miles before the canyon narrows and deepens and you enter the Upper Black Box. The rapids start out fairly easy. There is a great play spot at one of the first ones. There are several miles of Class 2 rapids with some being quite long.

Submarine Drop in the first Black Box of the San Rafael River.

When the rapids change character, turning into short steep drops of Class 3 to 4 difficulty, scout any that you can't see over. The whole river, in one of the early ones, drops into a narrow crack and falls about 10 feet. This must be portaged. We do it by landing on the right, putting in at the top of a long sloping rock, and sliding down into the river.

You will come to Submarine Drop about a mile below the portage. There's a great view from the top of the rock on the right. It's easy to disappear temporarily when you run this. The next rapid is in another half mile. A large boulder pile on the right squeezes the river left. A quick scout will help you pick the right line.

The canyon narrows even more and you will come to a spot where you can't see the bottom of a rapid. There is a good landing spot on the left. Get out there and scout. The main current runs into the right wall and is squeezed too narrow for a boat to fit. If there is enough water, about 500 cfs, the run is on the left side, twisting through narrow slots to the brink of the falls and dropping 10 feet into the pool below. If the water is too low, you will have to climb down or jump. Immediately after, the river funnels through a narrow slot on the left. This rapid is where boaters have had to climb out when the river was too high.

There is one more steep, narrow, twisting drop below the falls, which can and should be scouted. The river drops into a boulder in the middle and splits into slots on the right and left. Either can usually be run.

The river is squeezed even narrower as the cliffs lower, but stays smooth. You finally come out of the Upper Black Box into a wider canyon going around Mexican Mountain. It's about 2 miles back on an old road to where the road is blocked. If you were doing the run in two days and you didn't want to carry camping gear, you could leave your boats and walk back to the cars to sleep.

For the next 5.5 miles, the river loops around Mexican Mountain, offering small rapids to keep your interest up. The river finally cuts into the Coconino Sandstone again and the Lower Black Box begins. This is even narrower than the first. The water goes smoothly around a bend to the left and then, as it turns right, goes under Swasey's Leap. Supposedly Syd Swasey, riding his horse, leapt across the top of this narrow section of cliff, 50 feet above the river, to win a bet. The ancient wagon box bridge that identified the spot for a long time has fallen in.

Swasey's Leap marks the beginning of the rapid section. The lower box is only 3 miles long, but has more major rapids than the upper box. There are seven Class 3+ to 4 steep boulder-strewn rapids in the next 2 miles. The lower box has been run at flows above 1000 cfs. The rapids become Class 5. At flows above 400 cfs, some drops are difficult to stop above and so must be run blind. The large pools between rapids allow some recovery time, but the sheer walls don't allow getting out on the sides. Rescues must usually be done from another boat.

The Lower Black Box contains two big loops of the river and then opens slightly as the rock layers start tilting down. The river flows smoothly past some sulfur springs, then cuts through the San Rafael Reef in a wider but beautiful canyon. It then meanders through the flat desert and past the take-out above Black Dragon Wash, giving no inkling of the fury contained in the Black Boxes or the awesome beauty of the canyons.

The river meanders for another 42 miles of slow water and more open terrain until it joins the Green River.

≈ ≈ ≈ SEVIER RIVER

Map: See p. 136.

Difficulty: Class 1 to 3.
Length: 6 miles.
Average Gradient: 45 ft./mi.
Season: May-July, dam controlled.
Time: 2 hours.
Character: Small, meandering river through farmland in most sections. In the Big Rock Candy Mountain section, the river is steeper and in a canyon.
Levels: >250 cfs.
Elevation: Put-in 5800 ft., take-out 5550 ft.
Topo Maps: Marysvale.
Permits: No.
Shuttle Length: Same as run.
Access: U.S. 89 follows the river. About 25 miles south of Richfield.

The most popular section to run is just below Marysville and Big Rock Candy Mountain. Commercial trips are available there. The road follows the river, making scouting easy. The best drop is what's left from an old diversion dam. After a bridge at milepost 190, the river goes away from the road for a short distance and turns right. Where the river and canyon make a major left turn, the most difficult rapid starts (Class 3). The gauge is just below there. Normal peak flows and the best boating are at about 3.0 feet, though it can be run much lower. Take out before or at the next bridge. Continuing on involves low bridges, fences, and diversion dams.

OTHER SECTIONS

The Sevier is mainly flat and meandering, going through much open farm and grazing land. Several miles below Panguitch, the river goes into a canyon, picks up speed, and has a few Class 1 and 2 rapids. Watch out for fences and diversion dams. It's easiest to put in along U.S. 89 at about milepost 150 and take out on the bend just after milepost 155 or at the small dam about milepost 157.

A pleasant but long day run starts off I-15 where the road by Mills crosses the river. The take-out is just above the bridge where the river gets to Highway 132 at Leamington Canyon. There is a gauge on the left there with a short dirt road going to it. This is a 17-mile run of smooth water. There is no access between these points without trespassing. You will probably want 600 cfs or higher to get through in a day.

The river gradually picks up speed after the Highway 132 bridge and heads into Leamington Canyon. About 1.75 miles below the bridge, when the river is hidden from the road by a hill, you will come to a large diversion dam. Going off this would probably be fatal. The portage is not too bad on the right. Immediately below is a good rapid. A little over a mile away is a smaller dam. Scout and decide whether to run it. The river then heads toward the road where you encounter another small dam. Again, scout. The river stays fairly fast and goes under the railroad. It goes under it again in about a mile. After that, expect slower water, more meanders, channel splitting, and fences. A good take-out is in the town of Leamington off the only side road heading north. This is about a 10-mile run.

≈ ≈ ≈ SIXTH WATER

Map: See p. 49.
Difficulty: Class 4 to 5.
Length: 4 miles—all that's left.
Average Gradient: 215 ft./mi.
Season: Summer, dam release.
Time: 4 hours.
Character: Narrow, steep, boulders, log problems.
Levels: 250 to 400 cfs.
Elevation: Put-in 6320 ft. at Syar Tunnel, take-out 5620 ft.
Topo Maps: Two Tom Hill, Rays Valley.
Permits: No.
Shuttle Length: At least 12 miles.
Access: To get to the take-out, take U.S. 6 up Spanish Fork Canyon, turn
off at Diamond Fork, and drive to Three Forks. For the put-in, go
back to Spanish Fork Canyon and continue up on U.S. 6 to Sheep
Creek and turn left. Stay on the paved road until you've crossed Fifth
Water. You'll have to find your own way down to Sixth Water some-
where near the road for the Syar Tunnel. You could also continue up
Diamond Fork for 5.5 miles past Three Forks and take a dirt road
that takes you in 1.7 miles to another dirt road (Rays Valley Road) on
the right that will cross Sixth Water and eventually becomes the
paved road coming from Sheep Creek.

This is arguably the most challenging run in the state. Some of it is already gone. More of it may be gone in the near future. This is an unnatural river, created to bring water from the Green River drainage to the
east over to the west side of the Wasatch Mountains, mainly Utah Valley.
An old 1915 tunnel diverted water from Strawberry Reservoir and
dumped it into the Sixth Water Drainage, changing a stream that you
could step across into a raging river. A new tunnel has been built that
skips the top 6 miles of the run. Whether the top part will ever have
much water again, I don't know. It's very unlikely. In case there ever is, I've
included a description from the top. There are plans for putting the lower
part into a pipe, wiping out all boating.

Quotes are from Mark White's article in the May 1992 *Sports Guide* about our (Mark's, Roy Piskadlo's, and my) first full run. (A 2-mile section had already been run by Dave Hildebrand, Lane Johnson, Roy, and me that whetted our appetite.) Immediately below where the old tunnel dumps in, the river drops for a quarter mile at a rate of over 500 feet per mile. We chose to portage this section and named it "Unborn Soul." "Being located in an area full of religious overtones, the rapids seemed to beg for appropriate titles." I might add that standing by the first rapid with the ground literally shaking and the roar of the rapid in our ears, we suddenly felt more religious. There are several vertical drops in the next mile. We named the first "Visitors Center," since it gives an overview of what to expect. Through this section, you are really in a tributary of Sixth Water. Just before you enter the main canyon, there is an 8-foot falls. Since it introduces you to the official river and due to the likelihood that you will be totally immersed at the base of it, we called it "Baptism Falls."

Continuous rapids take you to "Mission Call," "a rather dangerous reversing ledge hole which will force unaggressive boaters into a tangled mess of overhanging willows. Roy spent a few tense moments communicating with his creator because he had not taken his mission call very seriously. Ten Percent Falls is another rapid that requires intricate maneuvering and waits a few miles downstream."

The river goes under a dirt road, offering access. It was 2 more miles of easier water to the new Syar Tunnel, where water now comes in from Strawberry Reservoir. From there on down, the river is still runnable until they put it in a pipe. Access is a problem. The road down to the tunnel is gated. Starting at the bridge upstream would require a 2.5-mile walk, so you'll have to figure your own way in.

The biggest falls (about 15 feet) is just below the Syar Tunnel. It has little warning but is a delightful treat to run, so we named it "Sister Jensen's Green Jell-O Surprise." Mark ran this first. "All went well, so Roy and Gary decided they too hungered for a heaping helping of Jell-O Surprise. With our adventure appetites momentarily satiated, we said thanks to Sis Jensen and headed downstream."

"Our next stop was the Celestial Gorge, which definitely held the run's most challenging, high stakes drops. . . . Only those who have repented for sins of sloppy technique should test their worthiness by running 'Pearly Gate Falls' and entering the Celestial Gorge." The river drops at a rate of 250 feet per mile through this gorge. The boulder-choked drops are often plugged with trees, so great care is required. Plan on lots of scouting.

When you get to the footbridge that leads to Fifth Water, the river eases from Class 5 to Class 4. A mile of rocky, log-filled drops takes you to Diamond Fork and the normal take-out. This is still dropping at a very respectable rate of 200 feet per mile. Roy had to walk this part because he tore a huge hole in his spray skirt, so we named it "Elder Roy's Road Show." A good test for the full run is to carry your boat up to the footbridge and run the lower mile. This also lets you scout on the way up. A rough trail also follows Sixth Water above the bridge, so you could continue on that and put in wherever you'd like.

≈ ≈ ≈ SMITH and MOREHOUSE CREEK

Map: See p. 24.
Difficulty: Class 2 to 3-.
Length: 5 miles + 2.5 on the Weber River.
Average Gradient: 100 ft./mi.
Season: June.
Time: 2 hours.
Character: Small mountain stream, fast, logs.
Levels: >150 cfs.
Elevation: Put-in 7600 ft., confluence with Weber River 7120 ft.
Topo Maps: Slader Basin, Hidden Lake.
Permits: No.
Shuttle Length: 7 miles.
Access: Take I-80 to the Wanship exit, go south on U.S. 189 to Oakley, follow the road (213) up Weber Canyon to the end of the pavement, and take the road to Smith & Morehouse Reservoir.

This is a fairly short run in a beautiful alpine setting. A road follows the upper part, so you can put in almost anywhere, except for a short section of private land. The first three-quarters of a mile is steepest, especially the cascading spillway. Then the river splits and slows a little as it goes past the campground. Right is usually best. After a quarter mile, it's back to mainly one channel and fast again for another half mile. You can expect occasional trees all the way across the river, so scout ahead of time or always have a place to land in sight. You will be paddling behind cabins once you go under the dirt road. There is a small drop when you go under the paved road (213). It's only a quarter mile from there to where you join the Weber River. You will need to paddle for about 2.5 miles on the Weber to get out at a bridge on the main road. The other bridges are all private.

≈ ≈ ≈ SNAKE RIVER

Milner Section

Difficulty: Class 1 to 5.
Length: 7 miles.
Average Gradient: 24 ft./mi.
Season: Dam release.
Time: 2 hours.
Character: Huge waves at high water, ledge drops in low water, basalt gorge.
Levels: >1500 cfs, has been run up to about 20,000 cfs.
Elevation: Put-in 4070 ft., take-out 3900 ft.
Topo Maps: Milner, Milner Butte, Murtaugh.
Permits: No.
Shuttle Length: 9 miles.
Access: I-84 between Burley and Twin Falls. Take exit 194. Follow the frontage road on the south side back east about a mile and turn south. Follow this to a "Y" and go left. Go right at the next "Y." Follow down to bridge below the dam. You can also go straight south from exit 194 about 3 miles to a "T." Left takes you in about 1.5 miles over to the other put-in route described. Right takes you to the take-out by going a mile west, then 1.2 miles south, then winding your way west for 2.5 miles, and then south to the steep road down to Star Falls.

This 9-mile section runs from just below Milner Dam to Star Falls. The first 1.5 miles are where you'll find all the excitement and most of the gradient. Scouting this section is a good idea. In low water there are separate rapids with the hardest being a 15-foot falls with a steep sneak on the right. At high water, this all becomes one long rapid with huge waves. At a narrow point, diagonal waves come off the side and converge into a huge curling wave that can stop a boat and flip it. A rafter was killed there a few years ago. The river then runs slow and smooth to Star Falls. A road comes in to the falls.

You might not notice Star Falls in high water until it's too late. Some Class 2 to 3 rapids lead into it and their noise covers the roar of the

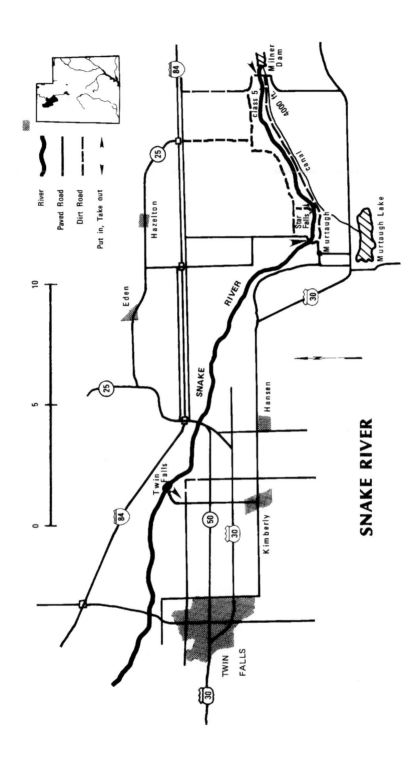

SNAKE RIVER

falls. The waterfall is right after a sharp right turn where the river drops about 15 feet into a huge hole and then about 20 feet over the main falls. It has been run at low flows but it's definitely a gamble as to what will happen to you. High water would probably be suicidal.

MURTAUGH SECTION

Difficulty: Class 2 to 4+.
Length: 13 miles of river, 1.3 lake.
Average Gradient: 27 ft./mi.
Season: Dam release.
Time: 4 to 6 hours.
Character: Basalt gorge, big waves at high water, big holes, ledge drops at low water.
Levels: >1200 cfs.
Elevation: Put-in 3880 ft., take-out 3515 ft.
Topo Maps: Murtaugh, Eden, Kimberly.
Permits: No.
Shuttle Length: 20 miles.
Access: The put-in can be reached by taking I-84 exit 188. Go south until you have to go east. Go east 1.2 miles and turn south and go to the bridge across the river. If putting in at Star Falls, go back north of the bridge about a mile, then east 1 mile, and south to the steep road down to the river. You may need four-wheel drive; or carry your boat a quarter mile. For the take-out, go back to I-84, head west, and take exit 182. Go south. As you cross hundreds of feet above the river, you can see Pair-A-Dice Rapid just upstream. After crossing the Snake River, head west on the first road for about 3 miles. Turn right and head north, dropping down to Twin Falls Park at the reservoir. It's about 3 miles shorter to go south from the Murtaugh Bridge and go through Murtaugh and Hansen to get to the take-out.

When there's water, this is a great run. You can get in a couple extra rapids by putting in right below Star Falls. You will get to run Amnesia and Basalt Falls. These are two of the best at high water. The more common put-in is at the Murtaugh bridge. There are many Class 3 to 4 rapids from there on down. At higher flows (above 8,000 cfs), the waves are Grand

Canyon size but usually straightforward. In very low flows, the drops become steeper and more technical. There are a number of great play spots. Rapids include Mabeline and Misty, and a mile or two above Hansen Bridge is a rapid called Junkyard (the reason for the name is obvious). Below this are Horseshoe Rapid and then the longest rapid, called Sine Waves.

Pair-A-Dice Rapid is just upstream from the Hansen Bridge where two islands block the river. Scout from the left bank or left island. The run is through the center chute. The right chute is a killer falls except at low flows, when it becomes runnable. At low flows, the water no longer goes left of the left island and a ledge is exposed between the two islands. At flows above 16,000 cfs, the rapid is often portaged. The left island offers the easiest portage. The center chute has some huge waves that can throw you into the ugly hydraulic below the falls on the right.

The river spreads out below the Hansen Bridge and has a ledge (called the Hooker) all the way across the river. Several chutes go through but it's hard to scout, so most boaters, at least the first time, run the far right side. Below this is Fantasy Island. You can land there to scout the next rapid, called Let's Make a Deal, a rapid with four basalt islands dividing the river into five slots. At high water, your choice may have dire consequences. Don't choose door number 4 or 5 without serious scouting. (Number 1 is on the left and 5 is on the right.) At low flows, some of the slots become too shallow. Doors 4½ and 5 are usually the choices at low flows.

Redshank and Duckblind Rapids are next. They become quite interesting at low flows. You may want to scout them. The last rapid, The Idaho Connection, has the finest surfing waves of the run at medium to high flows. The lake behind Twin Falls backs up to there. After 1.3 miles of paddling on the lake you will be at an access point on the left. Many paddlers put in at this take-out and paddle up the lake to play at The Idaho Connection when it's at its best.

≈ ≈ ≈ **SPANISH FORK RIVER**

Difficulty: Class 1 to 2+ (P).
Length: Up to 12.5 miles.
Average Gradient: 35 ft./mi.
Season: May, June.
Time: 1 to 4 hours.
Character: Small, fairly steady gradient, dams.
Levels: >300 cfs.
Elevation: Put-in 5000 ft., take-out 4640 ft.
Topo Maps: Billies Mountain, Spanish Fork Peak.
Permits: No.
Shuttle Length: About the same as run.
Access: U.S. 6 in Spanish Fork Canyon follows the river. A short side
  road on the south takes you up to the bottom of the Thistle slide.

You can run several sections or do the whole thing. Below the Thistle
slide, the river runs through three pipes. Put in just below. One and a half
miles of Class 1 and 2 take you to where Diamond Fork comes in. As the
Spanish Fork River gets low, more water is sent down Diamond Fork,
making their confluence a good spot to put in later in the year.

One of the better rapids is about a quarter mile below Diamond
Fork. The river gradually gets easier and becomes quite flat shortly after
passing Pole Canyon (also called Covered Bridge Canyon). The bridge at
Pole Canyon is the last easy place to exit without trespassing. It's about 2
more miles to a diversion dam where the only way out is to trespass
around the gatekeeper's house. A short private side road comes in to
this dam from U.S. 6.

It's rare to have enough water to run below this diversion dam.
When there is water, this is a fun stretch. The river is fast and narrow
with fairly continuous waves. As the canyon opens, you come to a diversion dam. After you portage around this, the river turns left and then right
and then starts narrowing down into a short canyon that cuts through a
bench area into the valley. This section contains many excellent Class 2
rapids, some boulders to dodge, and another diversion dam. Scout the
dam and decide if you want to run it. Immediately after, the river drops

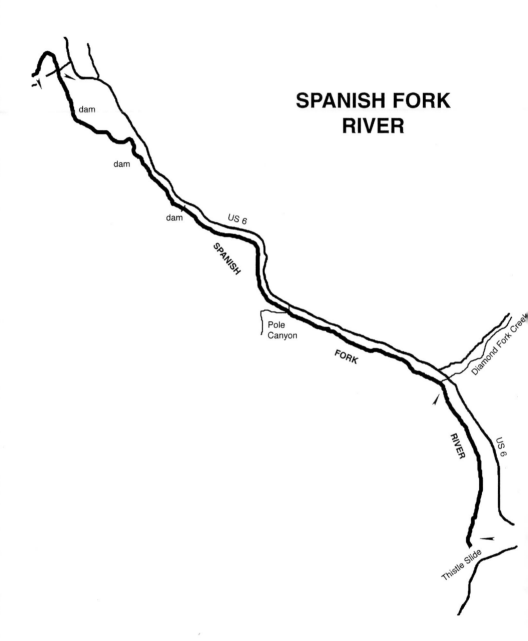

SPANISH FORK
RIVER

dam

dam

dam

US 6

SPANISH

Pole
Canyon

FORK

Diamond Fork Creek

RIVER

US 6

Thistle Slide

Spanish Fork River.

through some boulders (Class 2+). You shortly come to the road going from U.S. 6 by the Little Acorn Restaurant to the Spanish Oaks Golf Course. The bridge there is a good take-out, or continue for another mile around the golf course. Get out after the golf course when a canal comes in from the left. Right after this is a dangerous diversion dam.

Map: See p. 46.
Difficulty: Class 1 to 4+.
Length: 21 miles to Red Creek.
Average Gradient: 64 ft./mi.
Season: Late April to June.
Time: 5 to 6 hours.
Character: Narrow, rocky at times, remote in spots, alpine canyon transitioning to desert, logs, low bridges.
Levels: >200 cfs.
Elevation: Put-in 7350 ft., take-out 5940 ft.
Topo Maps: Strawberry Reservoir NE & SE, Strawberry Peak, Deep Creek, Fruitland, Avintaquin Canyon, Strawberry Pinnacles, Sams Canyon, Rabbit Gulch.
Permits: No.
Shuttle Length: About 28 miles, depending on where you get out.
Access: From U.S. 40, take the turnoff for Soldier Creek Dam and drive about 4.5 miles to the day-use area below the dam to put in. For the take-out follow U.S. 40 east about 14 miles to the turnoff for Red Creek and Strawberry Pinnacles. Follow this road 6 miles to the Strawberry River. There are several places to access the river both upstream and downstream.

I've tried to run this river again since writing the earlier edition of this book but have never caught it at the right level. The only change that I'm aware of is that much of the land through the narrow canyon was purchased by the Nature Conservancy and is thus protected from private development.

For about 8 miles below Strawberry Reservoir, the river runs in a beautiful, narrow, mountain canyon that seldom sees visitors. Even fishermen rarely venture more than a mile below the dam. No roads go all the way through. The only trail ends about 3 miles below the dam near Willow Creek Canyon.

The river flows past small meadows and over beaver dams, splashing against a few rocks, with the hardest sections being Class 2 for the first 2 miles. Near the confluence with Willow Creek, the gradient increases and the character of the river changes dramatically. Steep, narrow boulder drops replace the riffles. The trail ends, and this is your last chance to turn back.

You will encounter rockier Class 3 and 4 rapids. The many sharp turns can make it hard to see what's ahead. Scouting can usually be done by going from eddy to eddy. Always keep a landing spot in sight. Logs can block the whole river and portages can be difficult due to thick bushes and the steep sides of the narrow canyon.

After about 5 miles, the canyon opens some and the river eases a little, with longer straight stretches where you can make better time. Once you get to the dirt road, watch out for barbed-wire fences and low bridges. You are entering private land with many cabins.

The scenery changes from alpine to desert near Timber Canyon. The unique Strawberry Pinnacles tower near where Red Creek comes in. After Red Creek, the river is wider and straighter and the fences and logs are less of a problem. The best paddling ends where the road crosses the river about 4 miles below Red Creek. Several drops about a half mile above this bridge offer some excitement. There are about 11 more miles of slower and relatively smooth water to Starvation Reservoir. If you go all the way to Starvation, you will then have to paddle several miles across the lake to get to a take-out.

≈ ≈ ≈ **UINTA RIVER**

Map: See p. 194.
Difficulty: Class 1 to 3 (P).
Length: 9 miles.
Average Gradient: 85 ft./mi.
Season: May-July.
Time: 2 to 3 hours.
Character: Fairly small mountain stream, rocky, logs, diversion dams.
Levels: >300 cfs.
Elevation: Put-in 7600 ft. at Uinta Canyon Campground, take-out 6920 ft.
Topo Maps: Fox Lake, Bollie Lake, Heller Lake, Pole Creek Cave.
Permits: No.
Shuttle Length: Same as run.
Access: From U.S. 40 in Roosevelt, take Highway 121 west and then north. At Neola, keep heading north to the river. The road follows the river, so you can get in and out almost wherever you want. There are several campgrounds and picnic areas near the upper end of the road. The Uinta Canyon Campground gets you closest to the river.

This is one of the largest rivers coming out of the Uinta Mountains. Almost all its water is funneled off for power and irrigation at one point or another. There are about 9 miles that can be run from the Uinta Canyon Campground, just above Clover Creek, to the bridge below the Uinta Power Plant. The gradient is quite steady, with fast Class 2 to 2+ rapids. Splitting channels and logs are the greatest hazard, requiring Class 3 to 4 skills to stay out of trouble. There is a diversion dam just over 2 miles from the put-in, sending water into the Power Plant Canal. The road crosses in another mile for a possible access point. Then it's another 6 miles to the bridge below the power plant. Many canals drain the river below there.

A trail follows the Uinta River above the end of the road. If you are willing to carry your boat or get pack horses to do it, you can run quite a bit more of the river. Les Jones first ran this in 1974. Mark White and Jeff McFarlane did it recently and report a wonderful run in a narrower,

Packing for the upper Uinta River.
Photo by Mark White.

Upper Uinta River. Photo by
Mark White.

more exciting canyon. They rated it Class 3 to 4+ with continuous gradient, several rock gardens, and some bedrock slides. It's 11.5 miles from
the bridge over Shale Creek to Uinta Canyon Campground with an average gradient of 183 feet per mile. Ideal flow is around 600 cfs.

More information can be found at the website for the Virgin River Runners Coalition at www.virginriver.org. Consider joining this group. They have info on more than just the Virgin River, including links to river flows all over the west. You can also thank them for keeping the Virgin River open to boaters in Zion National Park.

NORTH FORK

Difficulty: Class 2 to 4+.
Length: 3.5 miles.
Average Gradient: 90 ft./mi.
Season: April-June.
Time: 2 hours.
Character: Beautiful desert canyon, steep, rocky, dams, logs.
Levels: Minimum by law for boating is 150 cfs, but over 250 cfs is better. >1.6 on gauge.
Elevation: Put-in 4320 ft., take-out 3840 ft.
Topo Maps: Temple of Sinawava, Springdale East.
Permits: Yes; fill out at visitors center. No limits at this time. Must also get a permit for your car if you want to drive your boats to the put-in.
Shuttle Length: Same as run. Use the park's shuttle buses.
Access: From I-15 near St. George, take Highway 17 past Toquerville to the turnoff for Springdale. Follow Highway 9 to Zion National Park. You will have to pay the park entrance fee. You can get to this same place from U.S. 89 by taking Highway 9 from Mt. Carmel.

The North Fork of the Virgin in Zion National Park offers incredible scenery as well as great paddling. The shuttle buses take care of shuttle hassles. Depending on how they are doing it, you will need either to get a red pass and drive your vehicle to your put-in, unload, drive your vehicle down to the parking area, and take the bus back up, or to load your boats on the shuttle bus from the parking area and be dropped off at your put-in.

VIRGIN RIVER

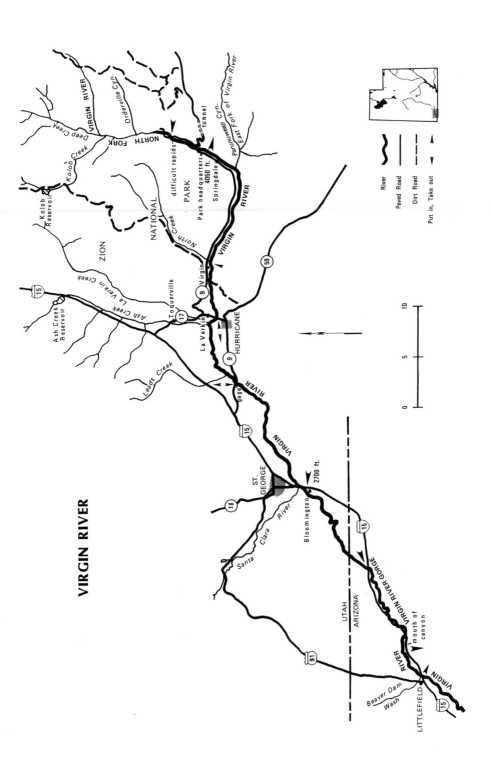

Virgin River, steep drops. Timpoweap Canyon. Photo by Rob Burton.

Virgin River in Zion National Park. Photo by Alan James.

If you start at the end of the road, you will have fairly easy water for 5 miles, until Court of the Patriarchs. The water drops over a little dam and changes character dramatically. You enter the hardest part of the park run as you go around the first corner. The first vertical drop is Corral Falls. Then you enter Satan's Staircase. At very high flows, this is pushing Class 5. At low flows, 200 to 300 cfs, it's Class 3+. The next 1.5 miles are continuous fun as you run through many boulder gardens. When you come to a huge slide on the right, get out and scout Landslide Rapid. The river is pinched between the highway and the slide. Boulders have been stacked across the river to slow it down. This has created some holes. Just above the highway bridge, there is a 5-foot sloping drop. Scout before running. A little below the bridge is another sloping drop that is usually portaged. The river is easier on down to the parking area by the visitor center.

The river appears to be Class 1 and 2 in the 20 miles from the end of the park to the town of Virgin. The dangers include diversion dams, fences, and logs. The land is almost all private.

VIRGIN TO LAVERKIN (Timpoweap Canyon)

Difficulty: Class 3 to 5+ (P).
Length: At least 3.2 miles.
Average Gradient: 90 ft./mi.
Season: April-June.
Time: 3 to 4 hours.
Character: Steep, tight, huge boulders, logs, dams, boulder sieves, deep canyon.
Levels: >200 cfs.
Elevation: Put-in 3400 ft., take-out 3040 ft.
Topo Maps: Virgin, Hurricane.
Permits: No.
Shuttle Length: 7 miles.
Access: Take Highway 9 or 17 from I-15 to the border between Hurricane and LaVerkin. The take-out is at Pah Tempe Hot Springs on the south side of the river and the east side of the road. The put-in is on one of the side roads off Highway 9 at or west of Virgin. See description below.

This challenging run was not totally destroyed by the Quail Creek Project. Access is a problem, though. You can put in wherever you can find access above the town of Virgin and paddle down to the dam diverting water to Quail Creek Reservoir. You can also take a side road at the west end of Virgin that crosses the river. The walls are vertical at the bridge, but if you take a small dirt road to the left, shortly after crossing the bridge, it takes you back upstream to a place where there aren't cliffs and you can put in.

Once at the dam, you will have to trespass to get around it. It's 30 feet off a cliff to get back in. The alternative is to walk down to a cut in the cliff and climb a tall chain-link fence topped with razor wire and put in a little ways below. There are some rough roads up on top that take you close to this area where you could climb down to start the trip, or possibly drive with four-wheel drive. This is the way I'd recommend, since it skips the flat-water above the dam and, I believe, the trespass problem. This description doesn't cover the short section that is immediately below the dam.

However you manage to get there, the hardest part of the entire Virgin River is about to begin. One hazard that isn't obvious is the sudden releases from the dam. Be aware that this can happen. Most of this 3.2-mile run is full of huge boulders. There are numerous sieves where a swim could mean you never surface. So don't be afraid to portage if you're not confident of making a move. It is also wise to do a lot of scouting. The run can be very fun and satisfying if you're careful. Don't forget to take time to enjoy the beauty of the deep gorge as well as the paddling. The hard rapids continue until just before the last bend above Pah Tempe Hot Springs. So the river looks pretty easy at the take-out. You will probably be charged a small fee to leave your car at the hot spring, but it's the only reasonable place to leave a car. It's also a pleasant soak after some hard paddling.

LaVERKIN TO S.R. 9 BRIDGE

Topo Maps: Hurricane, Harrisburg Junction.

This section starts at Pah Tempe Hot Springs. This 12.5-mile run is fairly easy, with some interesting gorges and enough whitewater to keep you

Virgin River Gorge. Photo by Jared Cieslewicz.

on your toes. Most of the land is private, so be respectful. The best rapid starts below the hot springs, just after going under the highway bridge. About 1.5 miles below the bridge, LaVerkin Creek and then Ash Creek come in on the right. You will need about 400 cfs to run this section.

BLOOMINGTON TO LITTLEFIELD (Virgin River Gorge)

Difficulty: Class 1 to 3+ (P).
Length: 33 miles.
Average Gradient: 20 ft./mi.
Season: April-June.
Time: 6 to 8 hours.
Character: Deep desert gorge, rocky, diversion dams, fences.
Levels: >300 cfs.
Elevation: Put-in 2500 ft., take-out 1900 ft.
Topo Maps: St. George, White Hills, Purgatory Canyon, Mountain Sheep Spring, Littlefield.
Permits: No.

Shuttle Length: About the same as run.
Access: I-15 south of St. George follows much of the river. See below.

Put in from the bridge crossing the river in Bloomington. There is a short drop soon after this. The broad valley you start in eventually narrows into a canyon. Sand waves liven things up at higher flows. It's about 7 miles to the "First Narrows." Beware of a new dam built as a fish barrier about a mile below this and after you go under some power lines. Watch for a warning sign. Portage on the right. The river stays mostly smooth with a few riffles and a rapid.

You come to the I-15 bridge about 13 miles below Bloomington. This is about milepost 23 and is a possible access point. Unfortunately, there is no freeway exit. Pull all the way off the road above the bridge to unload. Don't leave your vehicle there. Park on the other side of the bridge or use the dirt road on the other side of the freeway that cuts back to overlook the bridge (this requires going down to the rest area and turning around).

The section to the Cedar Pockets Rest Area is about 6.5 miles long. There are many rocky Class 2 and 3 drops starting with Pothole Rapid, then LA Freeway Rapid, Table Top Rapid, By-the-Pipe Rapid, Keyhole Rapid, New Forest Circus Follies, and Turtle Rapid. The canyon opens more and you have Go-for-the-Hole Rapid and Tree Rapid. A couple miles of easier water leads to the rest area take-out. This is a BLM fee area.

Below the rest stop, the river is fairly easy for a ways, and then the canyon narrows and the rapids become a little harder. Sullivan Canyon is a possible access point. There is a turnout on the northbound side of the freeway. Downstream is Dolphin Rapid below an arch on the north side that looks like a dolphin. Big 10 Falls is a fairly long rapid starting at the freeway bridge. A scout may be wise if you've never run this. The river makes a big curve to the left. There is a fairly abrupt drop near the end of this before going under the freeway again. The next mile of rapids is called The Back Nine. Warm springs come in along there and warm the river some.

Right before the canyon opens, rock fall brought in from the Quail Creek flood blocks the river, creating Let's Make a Deal. Logs usually block doors 1 and 2. Door 3 is usually good at medium to higher flows. You can portage on the right. Whorehouse Rapid, a long, fun, rocky rapid, immediately follows this.

The take-out can be a challenge. I've taken out immediately below Whorehouse Rapid and climbed the steep bank. About 2.5 miles below the mouth of the canyon is another place to take out. The parking area isn't visible from the river, so scout it out ahead of time so you can recognize the spot. This is accessible from the freeway on a dirt road that heads back up to a sidetrack that ends near the river. You can also continue down to Littlefield and climb out there. However, this may involve trespassing, so you may need to get permission.

≈ ≈ ≈ WEBER RIVER

Difficulty: Class I to 3 (P).
Length: Up to 28 miles.
Average Gradient: 65 ft./mi.
Season: May, June.
Time: I long day or short sections.
Character: Fast, continuous gradient, rocks, logs, bridges, fences, mountain stream, and private ranch land.
Levels: >300 cfs, best at 500 to 800 cfs.
Elevation: Put-in 7900 ft., take-out 6060 ft.
Topo Maps: Whitney Reservoir, Slader Basin, Hidden Lake, Hoyt Peak, Kamas, Crandall Canyon.
Permits: No.
Shuttle Length: About the same as run.
Access: East on I-80 from Salt Lake City to Wanship. Take U.S. 189 south. It parallels the river and offers direct access or side-road access. At Oakley, turn east on the Weber Canyon Road, which follows the river fairly closely. At Thousand Peaks Ranch, continue on the dirt road to the Holiday Park area for the highest put-ins. Most of this is private property.

This is a very beautiful stretch, running through Weber Canyon and then through farmland. The canyon part is full of summer homes. Almost all the land is private, so be careful where you put in and take out.

The highest you can put in without carrying your boat is the end of the road above Holiday Park. You may, however, want to put in a mile or so downstream after several forks of the river have come together.

The river is small, rocky, and swift in this upper part—mostly Class 2. The hazards are low bridges and logs. About a mile below the lower end of Holiday Park, the river enters a large, open meadow that is part of Thousand Peaks Ranch. It is mostly smooth through there but splits several times. You come to the low Thousand Peaks bridge and the river picks up some speed. It then gets smoother again as it goes through more meadow.

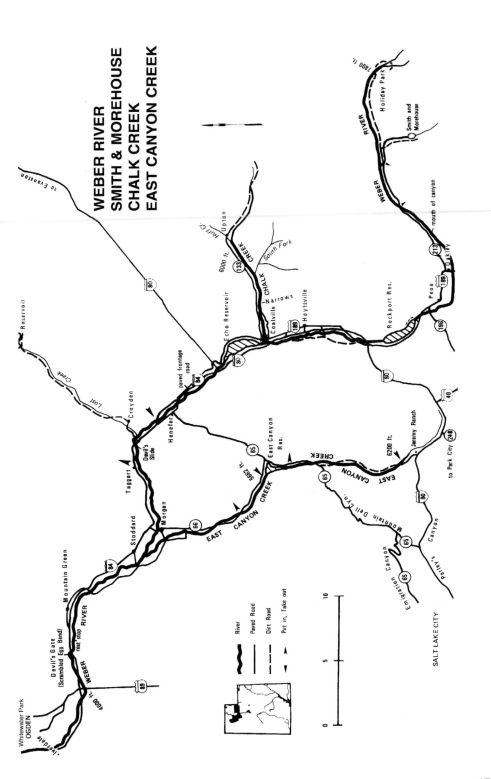

WEBER RIVER
SMITH & MOREHOUSE
CHALK CREEK
EAST CANYON CREEK

≈ 173

Upper Weber River.

A half mile upstream of the turnoff to Smith & Morehouse, the Weber becomes steeper and narrower and splits several times. The bank becomes wooded, creating great logjam danger. Scout any blind turns. You may need Class 4 skills to avoid logs and get through this stretch, especially in high water.

The worst is over after the next bridge unless there is barbed wire. The canyon opens up. Smith & Morehouse Creek enters in about 1.5 miles, adding much water. The river remains quite swift. There are a few good play spots at the right levels. Continue to watch out for trees in the river. There is a good access point where the river goes under the main road. This is about 10 miles below the Thousand Peaks bridge.

The river continues fast and Class 2. About a quarter mile above the mouth of the canyon is a gauge. Some good surfing waves are in this area. Shortly below is a possible access point. Below this, the river goes past the headgates for a canal. Shortly below is a road crossing, offering possible access. A mile below is a dam that needs portaging. Another mile takes you to an even larger dam with about a 15-foot drop onto cement.

Portage left. Water is diverted there to the Provo River through a large canal. Just below this is another road crossing and access point.

A little above the highway through Oakley (U.S. 189), the river breaks into many channels for a short ways, no channel being very big. After the bridge, the river is more open and has fewer logs. It's about 7 more miles to Rockport. Watch out for low bridges below. There is usually a good surf wave under one bridge. Just before coming to the west hillside, there is a cement wall and a drop at a dam. This can be runnable with good surfing at the right level.

The scenery changes when you get to the steep hills and cliffs on the west. The waves can be big and rolling at high water. A bridge for U-196 (Browns Canyon Road) crosses the river. There is a rocky dam below; it can usually be run on the right. The next bridge has a drop immediately below it. At higher levels, it offers some fun playing. This would be a possible access point. Below there, you have Rockport State Park on the right, where you can enter for a fee and camp. The bridge leading to the park is the last access point before getting to Rockport Reservoir.

ROCKPORT RESERVOIR TO ECHO RESERVOIR

Topo Maps: Wanship, Coalville.

This section is about 12 miles if you get out at the Coalville exit on I-80. Four other roads cross the river; all of them are good access points. Plan on 3 to 4 hours of boating time, and about 10 portages.

The run is mainly through farmland. However, in several sections, if you're not careful, you might find yourself in the driver's seat of an abandoned car, dumped in to protect the bank. These old cars are really the only things marring the view of cottonwoods, willows, and foothills. There are other challenges, however. Many obstacles make it less enjoyable and more dangerous than most stretches. Expect many barbed-wire fences, diversion dams, logjams, and overhanging bushes with sharp thorns. This is a popular fishing stretch.

ECHO THROUGH HENEFER

Difficulty: Class 1 to 2.
Length: 3 miles (9 from Echo Dam).

Average Gradient: 20 ft./mi.

Season: April to September.

Time: 1 to 2 hours.

Character: Farmland, small diversion dams, fences, a few rocks, occasional trees.

Levels: >250 cfs.

Elevation: Take-out 5260 ft.

Topo Maps: Coalville, Henefer.

Permits: No.

Shuttle Length: Same as run.

Access: Access is a problem for the upper part of this stretch. There are "no trespassing" signs on all the roads immediately below the dam. A frontage road offers access in a few places, but the highest points are now closed. This is an issue that needs to be addressed when the dam is relicensed. There is access in several places from about a mile above Henefer to the bridge at the east end of Henefer (freeway exit) as well as access at the next exit on the west end of Henefer.

If you can gain access below the dam, there is a river-wide drop just before going under the freeway. Decide for yourself if you want to run it. The run is about 9 miles to the west Henefer exit. There is a Class 2 rock garden above the first Henefer exit. The river winds past cottonwood trees and through farmland.

LOWER HENEFER EXIT TO TAGGART

Difficulty: Class 1 to 3-.

Length: 5.2 miles.

Average Gradient: 18 ft./mi.

Season: April to September.

Time: 1 to 3 hours.

Character: Fairly fast, several rock gardens, several play spots, bridges, unnatural due to freeway on one side and railroad on the other.

Levels: >250 cfs, best at >400 cfs.

Elevation: Put-in 5260 ft., take-out 5170 ft.

Topo Maps: Devils Slide.

Permits: No.

Shuttle Length: Same as run.

Access: I-84 parallels it; access at exits.

This 5-mile stretch is the most popular run on the Weber. Easy access is found along the short side road at the west Henefer exit. The river gets pinched between the freeway and the railroad in about a quarter mile. A Class 2+ to 3- rock garden for three-quarters of a mile is the result. Strong eddy lines create great spots to work on eddy turns and vertical moves. Total novices will find this section quite challenging. A number of inexperienced canoeists have destroyed their boats here.

After the rock garden and just before the bridges at the Croyden exit, there are some waves and a good eddy line. Watch out for the bridges just below. The pillars can pin a boat and high water may not leave enough clearance. The upstream side of the bridge is a possible access point. The next major bend to the left has some rocks and sometimes hides fallen trees. A good pop-up spot forms at high water there. Below, the river goes under the freeway.

An easier rock garden begins below the bridge in the area of Devil's Slide. There is a play wave at the end of this. There are several short drops that offer some playing before the river enters the Freeway Slalom Rapid, where the river goes under the freeway and boaters must dodge quite a few pillars as they bounce through the waves. There's a fairly straight shot if you stay in the middle. A few boats have pinned on the pillars with at least one person almost dying. So beginners need to be careful. A railroad bridge above Taggart Falls warns of your approach to this rapid. A play spot forms at most levels on the left at the end of the rapid. The lower right side is a rocky shelf that turns into an ugly hole at high flows. The take-out is below on the right. There is a small store and restaurant at the freeway exit. You might even be able to pay someone there to do a shuttle.

TAGGART TO REST STOP BELOW MOUNTAIN GREEN

Topo Maps: Devils Slide, Morgan, Peterson, Snow Basin.

This 21-mile stretch is seldom run. One of the problems is that often much of the water is diverted partway through the run. I have seen quite a bit of wildlife in this section, including a number of bald eagles.

After Taggart, the river goes under the freeway to the north side and then back to the south side. In another quarter mile, just before the canyon opens into Round Valley, there is a usually runnable, 2-foot, boulder-drop dam. The river winds through the valley and then the canyon narrows. Just before it widens, about 3.5 miles from the last diversion dam, the river goes against the left wall where there is a road and then makes a right turn just before a bigger diversion dam with an ugly reversal. This should be scouted. It can be run at some levels in the right spot.

In another quarter mile, you will come to a diversion dam with a 6-foot drop that should be portaged. You are going through Morgan at this point. It isn't far to still another boulder dam with a 4-foot drop. Scout and decide whether to portage. Several roads crossing the river in Morgan could be used for access.

From the main road through Morgan it is about 3 miles of fairly smooth sailing to the next bridge—for the road between Stoddard and Milton. Unfortunately, all four sides of the bridge are fenced and have "no trespassing" signs. I suspect there is a county right-of-way that would allow access there, but you're on your own. Less than a mile from this bridge is the new large Stoddard Diversion Dam. This one's cement and metal, not boulders. You'll have to portage. There's no easy way around. You will have to climb fences. If you are going to paddle past Morgan, make sure there's water at Peterson, as this dam can divert most of the water. It's about 4.5 more miles to the bridge by Peterson, where there is good access. There are two small rock diversion dams in that stretch.

It is about 6 miles from Peterson, where there's freeway access, to the rest stop. About a quarter mile past Peterson, there is a rocky drop that is usually runnable if not plugged by debris. Five miles of fairly easy water, blocked in one spot by a fairly permanent-looking tree, will get you to an old bridge. Just below, some of the diverted water comes back in. There is a train bridge by the Mountain Green exit where there is potential access. There is a short rapid immediately below the train bridge and then one more mile of slow water to the rest area. The water backs up behind an unrunnable dam. Do not go past the rest area unless you are ready for Class 4+ rapids.

Scrambled Egg Bend (Devil's Gate) to Mouth of Canyon

Difficulty: Class 3 to 4+ (P).
Length: 3 miles.
Average Gradient: 80 ft./mi.
Season: Depends on irrigation needs.
Time: 1 to 2 hours.
Character: Steep, fast, rocky, holes, logs, dams.
Levels: >400 cfs.
Elevation: Put-in 4790 ft., take-out 4560 ft.
Topo Maps: Peterson, Ogden.
Permits: No.
Shuttle Length: Same as run.
Access: I-84 follows. About 3 miles east of U.S. 89, turn off at the rest area from the eastbound lanes of the freeway and drive down to the dam. Walk downstream a short ways to put in. From the westbound lanes, there is room to pull off the freeway shortly after crossing over the river at Scrambled Egg Bend. Drive up the dirt road to Scrambled Egg Bend. You may have to walk partway to get to the top of the rapid. Take out at the power plant or the mouth of the canyon. There is a dirt turnout from eastbound I-84 just east of U.S. 89 with a fisherman gate through the fence and another similar spot about a quarter mile farther east giving access to the lower diversion dam.

About a quarter mile below the dam at the rest stop, the river picks up speed and enters Scrambled Egg Bend. I believe it got this name from an egg truck that didn't quite make the turn on the old highway. The maps show it as Devils Gate. As the river turns right, it funnels into a narrow channel at the head of this long horseshoe bend. There's a cliff on the left and a concrete wall on the right supporting the old highway.

Expect big waves and holes in high water, rocks and chutes at lower levels. The river cuts left and widens as it drops through a steep boulder section of Class 4 to 4+ difficulty. You get a slight break as the river goes under a train bridge. You then have a series of three holes created by cement blocks. These were put in to help keep the river from undercutting the freeway. Scout this whole area before running. Logs have occasionally been a problem. People have been hurt, and a few killed, in this rapid; so don't take it too lightly. A swim is ugly and the unnatural rocks are very unfriendly.

The river eases to Class 3 but is still very fast, with few eddies and lots of rock dodging at low water down to the power plant. Diverted water comes in from the power plant, creating a fun play spot at some levels. If the gates at the power plant dam are down, you will have to portage. If they are open, scout to make sure the drops are clear and runnable. The right side is usually the safest.

After the power plant, the rapids continue for a quarter mile, slowing some just above a dangerous diversion dam. Portaging is probably easiest on the right. Many people exit here. The river continues swift but easier to U.S. 89.

MOUTH OF CANYON (U.S. 89) TO OGDEN

Difficulty: Class 1 to 3.
Length: 5 to 10 miles.
Average Gradient: 30 ft./mi.
Season: Depends on irrigation needs.
Time: 1 to 2 hours.
Character: Fast, wooded, dams, fences, logs.
Levels: >400 cfs.
Elevation: Put-in 4560 ft., take-out 4390 ft.
Topo Maps: Ogden.
Permits: No.
Shuttle Length: About the same as run.
Access: I-84 follows it. Access at interchanges and exits between U.S. 89 and Riverdale. There are also many dirt pullouts along the run from the westbound side of I-84 below U.S. 89 or eastbound I-84 just above U.S. 89.

The freeway parallels the river, but the cottonwoods and willows mostly screen it from view. A quarter mile below U.S. 89, where the on-ramp to westbound I-84 crosses, there are a couple of drops that make great surfing waves at high water. You can pull off to the side of the on-ramp and play. There are a couple more surf waves in the next mile. The river splits and spreads out in places, making it hard to run in low water. Watch out for trees.

You need to watch out for a drop immediately below where the road from the Uintah Exit crosses (not the toll road but the one heading upstream). This is an unnatural drop with cement blocks that should be scouted. At the right level and if it isn't full of trees, it can be run. The landowners on the sides of it don't appreciate boaters walking around it. Be quick and polite and apologize if they catch you. Confrontation will just make it harder for everyone else.

There are two easy drops by the "Riverdale exit, 1 mile" sign. These drops used to be much harder but were altered about two years ago. There is a big turnout there, making this a good take-out.

The river continues through Riverdale and Ogden (with parkways along parts and a couple of drops) for 4.5 miles to a new whitewater park that was recently built. This play spot has several drops set up in a way that as the river goes up or down, there are always places to surf, cartwheel, pop up, or enjoy whatever you'd like to do. Minimum flow is about 200 cfs. To get to this park, take 24th Street from I-15, turn north at B Avenue (550 West), turn east on the first street. The whitewater park is where it crosses the river. This is just west of all the railroad tracks.

Difficulty: Class 1 to 2.

Length: 37 miles Rangely to Bonanza, 34 more to BLM access.

Average Gradient: 7 ft./mi.

Season: April to early July, later in some years.

Time: 2 days Rangely to Bonanza, 2 more to BLM access.

Character: Fairly remote canyon, good current, no major drops, logs, nice camping, sheep.

Levels: >300 cfs.

Elevation: Put-in 5200 ft., take-out 4650 ft.

Topo Maps: Rangely (CO), Banty Point (CO), Walsh Knolls (CO), Weaver Ridge, Southam Canyon, Asphalt Wash, Archy Bench, Redwash SW, Ouray SE, Ouray.

Permits: No, but if you will be using Indian land such as exiting at the Mountain Fuel bridge, you need a permit from the Ute Indian tribe, P.O. Box 190, Fort Duchesne, UT, 84026.

Shuttle Length: Rangely to the Bonanza Bridge is about 31 miles. Bonanza Bridge to the BLM take-out is about 21 miles.

Access: Take U.S. 40 to U-88, the road west of Vernal going to Ouray, to get to the confluence with the White and Green Rivers. For the Bonanza area and BLM take-out, continue on U.S. 40 through Vernal and Naples. At the end of Naples, where the road turns east, turn south on a road signed for Bonanza (Highway 45). The road crosses the Green River in a few miles. Continue on past Bonanza and drop into the White River Canyon. Most start their trip under the bridge. For the BLM take-out, go back to Bonanza, turn west on the road for Ouray and the Mountain Fuel bridge. This soon turns into a dirt road (which gets quite bad in a heavy rain). Follow signs toward the Mountain Fuel bridge and then signs for the BLM river access. To get to Rangely from Bonanza, go east on a paved road across from the turnoff to the Mountain Fuel bridge. Follow this to Highway 64 and go southeast to Rangely.

The White River is still a wonderful run, but development is encroaching on it. Both homes and oil wells are changing the views. Fortunately, quite a bit of it is still fairly free of this. The dam that threatened it a few years

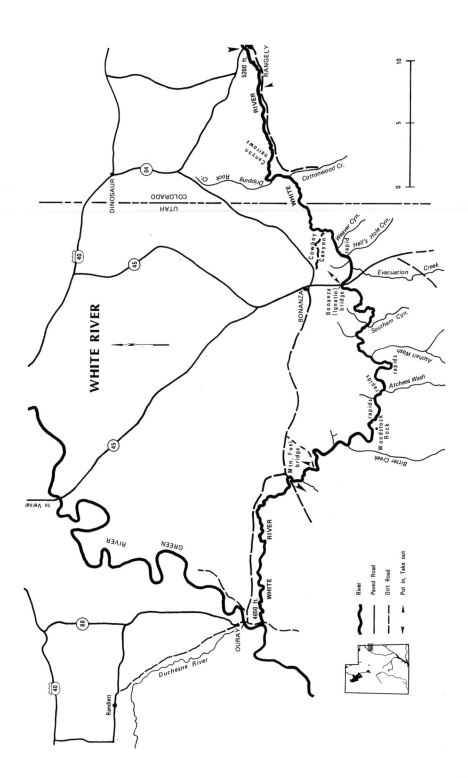

WHITE RIVER

River
Paved Road
Dirt Road
Put in, Take out

≈ 183

White River.

ago was put off as the price of oil dropped. With new threats of short-ages, this dam proposal could be revived. Be aware. To find out more about protecting it, contact the Uintah Mountain Club in Vernal.

The river starts in the Colorado Rockies. After leaving the moun-tains it becomes a meandering river with excellent camping among the cottonwoods. Fossils and petrified wood can be found in places. There are many small arches and windows in the cliffs of the canyon. The lush river bottom provides food, water, and shelter from the hot desert, mak-ing it a haven for beaver, wild horses, deer, eagles, and geese. At certain times it is also a haven for flies and mosquitoes. Be careful in the spring around the nesting geese or their babies.

Trips can range from a long day at high water to over a week, de-pending on where you get in and out. Hazards at low water are mainly rocks and shallows. At most levels, the biggest hazards are trees that have fallen in and block the channel.

You could put in at the bridge in Rangely where the main road crosses the river, but there isn't a very good place to pull off the road. A better place is in a park through town to the east. This will add about a mile to the trip. The first several miles really meander through the valley with mainly flat water. If you want to skip this, there is a public access point about 5 miles down River Road (the first road on the south side of the river heading west). This may be the only public access along this road. Many homes have now been built along it.

Ten miles of fairly smooth water from the public access point on River Road take you to where the valley and private homes end. The scenery improves and there are places to camp. There are signs in places marking public and private land. The river heads north briefly and then makes a 180-degree turn to go south. It's about 10 miles from there to Cowboy Canyon. A road comes in there but access has been closed, at least temporarily. So don't count on being able to use Cowboy Canyon to get in or out. About 4 miles below Cowboy Canyon is Hells Hole Rapid, a fairly long Class 2 rapid. The river continues swiftly with occasional small rapids for 3 more miles to the Bonanza Bridge.

The put-in by Bonanza is, at least temporarily, under the new bridge. Cross to the south side of the bridge, go a couple hundred yards, and make a 180-degree turn to the right to get under the bridge. There is a parking area with a couple tables. The river is mainly smooth below the bridge. About 3 miles down is an area that always seems to have logs blocking much of the river. It's about 9 miles from the bridge to where the dam was going to be built. A rough road comes in just upstream on the right. There are usually some major logjams in the area.

The river hits its most southerly point at about mile 15.5 from Bonanza. There are a few riffles in the area. Atchees Wash comes in on the left at about mile 20. Starting there and for the next 5 to 6 miles, you will find the most whitewater. At flows of around 700 to 1200 cfs, they are easiest. At low flows, they are quite rocky. At high flows, above 2000 cfs, the waves start getting fairly big and a few holes develop. Saddletree Draw comes in on the left in this section at mile 22. About 1.5 miles farther, as you start a bend to the left, is Woodstock Rock (named after the Peanuts comic-strip bird) on a ridge to the left.

A couple of aboveground pipelines come in about mile 27. The canyon starts opening up some. The new BLM take-out is on the right at about mile 34. There is a sign there marking it. Make sure you can recognize it in case the sign is torn down. There is a bathroom and camping area there.

Four more miles take you to the Mountain Fuel bridge. You will have to pay the Ute Tribe to take out there. Another 20 miles of flat water and more open canyon take you to the Green River.

Willow Creek.

≈ ≈ ≈ WILLOW CREEK

Map: See p. 120.
Difficulty: Class 3 to 5.
Length: 4 miles.
Average Gradient: 140 ft./mi.
Season: May, June.
Time: 3 to 4 hours.
Character: Steep, tight, boulders, falls, logs.
Levels: 75 to 200 cfs.
Elevation: Put-in 7040 ft., take-out 6480 ft.
Topo Maps: Helper, Matts Summit.
Permits: No.
Shuttle Length: Same as run.
Access: From U.S. 6 north of Price and in the coal mining area, turn off on U.S. 191 going to Duchesne. This road follows Willow Creek.

Most people who have seen this don't believe me that it can be run. Bushes have filled its bed. Usually you can step across it. It's one of those rivers that might have enough water only once every 20 years. When it does, it's an outstanding creek run.

There is a gauge just above Deep Canyon. About 1.5 miles above the gauge, two other streams join Willow Creek. This is the first place there is enough water to run. Put in anywhere in this stretch. From the stream junction to the gauge is fairly easy. There are a couple small drops above the gauge and a 4-foot drop at the gauge. The river becomes steep and rocky from there on. The biggest drop is a sloping falls that drops 15 feet in about 25 feet. Much of the river can be eddy scouted, but when you can't tell what's there, get out and scout. Watch out for logs. This is definitely a run for a short blunt creek boat.

When you come to an overhang, get out and scout the next several drops. There was a 5-foot falls that crashed onto a rock that we portaged. There are many more rocky drops in the next 2 miles. Take out where the river goes under the road. Check for a fence just above the bridge. Immediately below the bridge is an almost guaranteed pin. We haven't run below there. It's another 2.5 miles to the Price River, half of which goes through the coal mining area.

≈ ≈ ≈ YAMPA RIVER

CROSS MOUNTAIN

Difficulty: Class 3 to 5.
Length: 3 miles.
Average Gradient: 65 ft./mi.
Season: April to June.
Time: 2 to 3 hours.
Character: Huge boulders, tight turns, holes, logs, deep canyon.
Levels: >500 cfs.
Elevation: Put-in 5800 ft., take-out 5640 ft.
Topo Maps: Peck Mesa, Cross Mountain Canyon, Twelve Mile Mesa.
Permits: No.
Shuttle Length: 11 miles on the road, or walk 3 miles along the rim of the canyon.
Access: To get to the put-in follow U.S. 40 into Colorado. Continue about 8 miles east of Elk Springs and turn onto the signed road for Deerlodge Park. Follow this 4 miles to a parking area near the canyon mouth. To get to the put-in go back out to U.S. 40, go east almost 2 miles, and turn left on the dirt Moffat County Road 85. In 2 miles, the main road curves right; go left. In a quarter mile, the road splits again. Either will get you to a put-in. Right gives you a little longer run and more warm-up.

This is a short, deep, and spectacular canyon where the river cuts through the mountain instead of going around it. The rapids won't disappoint you. They match the ruggedness of the canyon. This is by far the most difficult section of the Yampa River.

The rapids begin shortly after you enter the canyon. Between 500 and 2000 cfs, the river is extremely good technical paddling but not overly difficult, mainly Class 3 to 4-. The waves aren't huge but the maneuvering is very tight through narrow slots, around giant boulders, over ledges, twisting through "S" turns—a magnificent run in a unique canyon. Rafts probably do better at 1500 to 4000 cfs—but only self-bailers. Above 4000 cfs, the river gets quite pushy. Flows above 6000 require serious big-water skills and paid-up life insurance. It is not usually run above about 12,000 cfs.

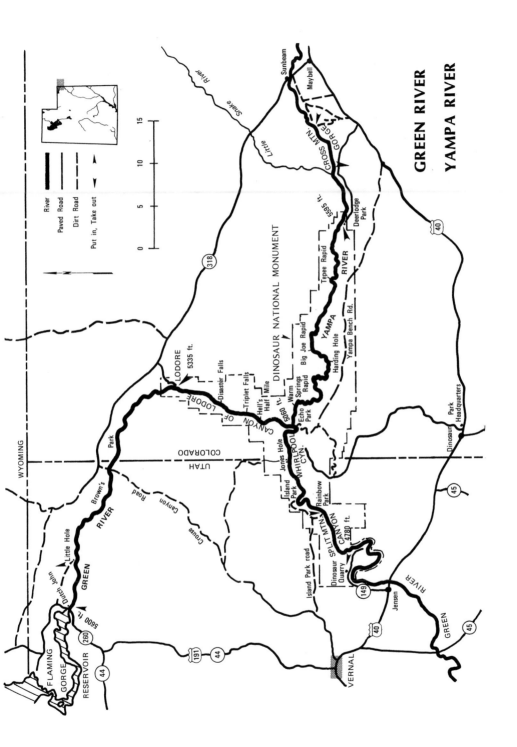

GREEN RIVER
YAMPA RIVER

≈ 189

Cross Mountain Gorge of the Yampa River.

The first few rapids are the most difficult, beginning with Mammoth Falls (Osterizer). This turns into a river-wide hole at high flows that most people will want to stay out of. The next major rapid is The Snake Pit. Rapids continue all through the canyon, and then you suddenly break out of the narrow walls into a big valley and smooth water.

DEERLODGE PARK TO THE GREEN RIVER

Difficulty: Class 1 to 4.
Length: 46 miles + 25 on the Green River.
Average Gradient: 11 ft./mi.
Season: Late April-June.
Time: 3 to 5 days.
Character: Fairly fast desert river, mostly just riffles, beautiful canyon, great camping.
Levels: >1000 cfs; canoes and kayaks can go down to about 500 cfs.
Elevation: Put-in 5600 ft., take-out 4780 ft. at Split Mountain.
Topo Maps: Indian Water Canyon, Haystack Rock, Tanks Peak, Zenobia Peak, Hells Canyon, Canyon of Lodore South.
Permits: Yes: NPS, Dinosaur National Monument, (970) 374-2468, http://www.nps.gov/dino/planyourvisit/privateriverrafting.htm.
Shuttle Length: 90 miles.
Access: To get to the put-in follow U.S. 40 into Colorado. Continue about 8 miles east of Elk Springs and turn onto the signed road for Deerlodge Park. Follow this 14 miles to the put-in. Most people take out at the Split Mountain boat ramp on the Green River (see that section). You could also take out at Echo Park, reached by a dirt side road to U.S. 40 that is impassable when really wet.

From Deerlodge Park, the portal to Yampa Canyon is visible. This is one of the most scenic canyons in Dinosaur National Monument. It cuts through Blue Mountain, the easternmost spur of the Uinta Mountains. For 45 miles you are in this deep canyon composed mainly of Weber Sandstone and the Morgan Formation.

If you're lucky, you may see bighorn sheep. You will see hoodoos, picturesque Harding Hole, and serpentine bends below Harding Hole where you travel 7 miles to cover 2 straight miles. Castle Park and Mantle Ranch are 12 miles above the confluence. This is the only car access in

Warm Springs Rapid on the Yampa River. Photo by Kirk Nichols

Yampa Canyon; however, the road is private. Just below is Mantle Cave, where evidence of pre-Columbian Indians of the Fremont culture has been found. Some of the best displays of desert varnish (manganese and iron oxide stains left from water evaporating off the cliffs) can be seen at Tiger Wall.

The river is mostly smooth but fast water. There are three major rapids: Tepee, Big Joe, and Warm Springs. Tepee is 8 miles from the canyon entrance. The next 2.5 miles after that are one of the fastest stretches of the river. Big Joe Rapid is halfway through the canyon, about 21 miles from the entrance. Warm Springs Rapid is just over 4 miles upstream from the confluence with the Green River. Several smaller rapids appear in low water.

Until 1965, there was no Warm Springs Rapid, only a riffle. On the night of June 10, a flash flood in Warm Springs Draw sent tons of rock and gravel into the river. The most difficult rapid in the canyon was formed and made worse later by slabs of rock falling from the left cliff. The next day two raft parties approached, unaware of what had happened. The first boatman was killed. His passengers made it through, but he was thrown from the raft and wasn't found for several days.

Warm Springs Rapid is long and fairly technical. In high water the waves are huge and the current draws everything toward giant holes— holes that have flipped the largest rafts. In a kayak, under experienced hands, the rapid is not too difficult because of the great maneuverability of these small craft; but in a waterlogged raft, the precise maneuvering for a clean run can be difficult. A self-bailing raft makes it much easier.

The last 4 miles are slow but scenic before the Yampa joins the Green River at Echo Park.w

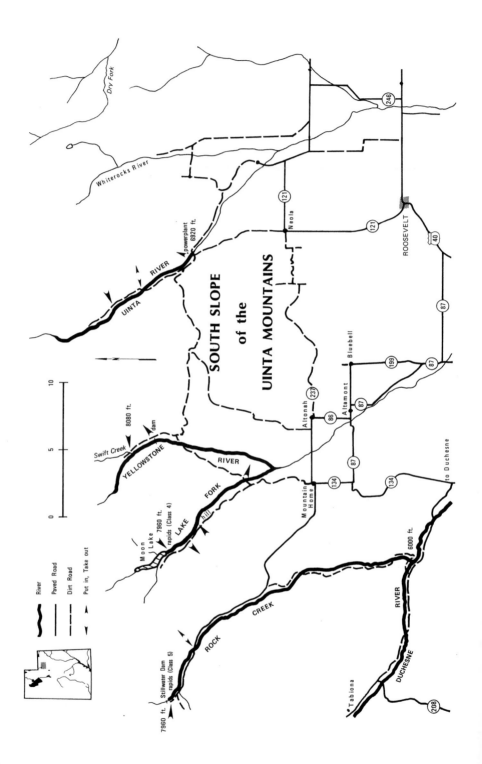

SOUTH SLOPE
of the
UINTA MOUNTAINS

≈ ≈ ≈ YELLOWSTONE RIVER

Difficulty: Class 1 to 2+.
Length: 2.2 miles.
Average Gradient: 100 ft./mi.
Season: Late May-June.
Time: 1 hour.
Character: Small, continuous mountain stream, logs.
Levels: >200 cfs.
Elevation: Put-in 8080 ft., take-out 7863 ft.
Topo Maps: Burnt Mill Spring.
Permits: No.
Shuttle Length: Same as run.
Access: From Duchesne and U.S. 40, take U-134 north to Mountain
   Home. Follow the signs toward Moon Lake. Watch for the signed
   road to the Yellowstone River and drive to the end of the road at
   Swift Creek Campground to put in. Take out at Reservoir
   Campground.

This is a very scenic and wooded stretch of river. The beautiful trees also
mean great logjam potential. The river is fast, with Class 1 to 2+ rapids.
About three-quarters of the way through the run, the river splits several
times. High water and beaver have teamed to down many trees and
block all the channels for about a hundred yards. The run ends shortly
afterward on the small reservoir.

Several other sections offer possible runs.

INTERNATIONAL SCALE OF RIVER DIFFICULTY
OF THE AMERICAN WHITEWATER AFFILIATION

Class 1: Easy. Fast-moving water with riffles and small waves. Few obstructions, all obvious and easily missed with little training. Risk to swimmers is slight; self-rescue is easy.

Class 2: Novice. Straightforward rapids with wide, clear channels that are evident without scouting. Occasional maneuvering may be required, but rocks and medium-sized waves are easily missed by trained paddlers. Swimmers are seldom injured and group assistance, while helpful, is seldom needed.

Class 3: Intermediate. Rapids with moderate, irregular waves that may be difficult to avoid and that can swamp an open canoe. Complex maneuvers in fast current and good boat control in tight passages or around ledges are often required; large waves or strainers may be present but are easily avoided. Strong eddies and powerful current effects can be found, particularly on large-volume rivers. Scouting is advisable for inexperienced parties. Injuries while swimming are rare; self-rescue is usually easy but group assistance may be required to avoid long swims.

Class 4: Advanced. Intense, powerful, but predictable rapids requiring precise boat handling in turbulent water. Depending on the character of the river, it may feature large, unavoidable waves and holes or constricted passages demanding fast maneuvers under pressure. A fast, reliable eddy turn may be needed to initiate maneuvers, scout rapids, or rest. Rapids may require "must" moves above dangerous hazards. Scouting is necessary the first time down. Risk of injury to swimmers is moderate to high, and water conditions may make self-rescue difficult. Group assistance for rescue is often essential but requires practiced skills. A strong Eskimo roll is highly recommended.

Class 5: Expert. Extremely long, obstructed, or very violent rapids that expose a paddler to above-average endangerment. Drops may contain large, unavoidable waves and holes or steep, congested chutes with complex, demanding routes. Rapids may continue for long distances between pools, demanding a high level of fitness. What eddies exist may be small, turbulent, or difficult to reach. At the high end of the scale, several of these factors may be combined. Scouting is mandatory but often difficult. Swims are dangerous, and rescue is difficult even for experts. A very reliable Eskimo roll, proper equipment, extensive experience, and practiced rescue skills are essential for survival.

Class 6: Extreme. One grade more difficult than Class 5. These runs often exemplify the extremes of difficulty, unpredictability, and danger. The consequences of errors are very severe, and rescue may be impossible. For teams of experts only, at favorable water levels, after close personal inspection and taking all precautions. This class does *not* represent drops thought to be unrunnable, but may include rapids that are only occasionally run.

DIFFICULTY RATING

Difficulty is very subjective. These are rough divisions and can change dramatically with different flow levels. There can be quite a bit of difference within a category. The divisions are for a whole section of river. An individual rapid may be harder and thus require portaging if you are at your maximum level. Changing hazards such as logs can also increase the difficulty. Please read the pertinent section for more detail.

Beginner

Bear River—most parts not described in this book.
Colorado River—Cisco to Dewey Bridge, just below Big Bend to the
    confluence with the Green River.
Dirty Devil River—the remoteness makes this an advanced-beginner run.
Green River—Brown's Park, Labyrinth and Stillwater Canyons.
Jordan River—Utah Lake to the Narrows, north of 3900 South.
Logan River—below Logan to Cutler Reservoir.
San Rafael River—Little Grand Canyon.
Sevier River—Mills section and most sections not described.

Intermediate

Bear River—Oneida Narrows.
Big Cottonwood Creek—below Cottonwood Mall.
Blacks Fork—most sections.
Blacksmith Fork—upper section.
Chalk Creek.
Colorado River—Horsethief and Ruby Canyons, Hittle Bottom to Big
    Bend (low water).
Currant Creek.
Diamond Fork.
Dolores River—Slick Rock to Gateway.
East Canyon Creek.
Fremont River—along the road in Capitol Reef National Park.
Green River—Flaming Gorge to Browns Park, Desolation and Gray
    Canyons.

Jordan River—Narrows to 3900 South.

Little Cottonwood Creek—below 900 East.

Mammoth Creek—section described.

Muddy Creek.

Ogden River—in town.

Price River—town of Price to the Green River.

Provo River—most sections.

San Juan River.

Sevier River—Big Rock Candy Mountain section, Leamington Canyon.

South Fork of the Ogden River.

Uinta River—most sections along the road.

Virgin River—lower part of Zion National Park to Quail Creek diversion dam, LaVerkin to I-15; below I-15 is advanced intermediate.

Weber River—most sections.

Yampa River—except high water.

Yellowstone River—logs may make it advanced.

Logan River—through town.

Advanced

Beaver Creek.

Blacksmith Fork—most of it.

Bruneau and Jarbidge Rivers.

Coal Creek.

Colorado River—Westwater Canyon and Cataract Canyon.

Cottonwood Creek.

Dolores River—Bradfield Recreation Site to Slick Rock, Gateway to Colorado River.

Duchesne River—Cataract Gorge on the North Fork.

Ferron Creek—part along road, almost intermediate level.

Green River—Lodore Canyon.

Huntington Creek—most sections at low to medium flows.

Lake Fork—low to medium flows.

Little Cottonwood Creek—below the mouth of canyon to 900 East.

Logan River—in the canyon.

Ogden River—canyon section at lower flows.

Price Canyon.

Provo River—Bridal Veil Falls section.

Rock Creek.

Salina Creek—most sections.

San Rafael River—Black Boxes.

Snake River—Murtaugh section.

Strawberry River—above Red Creek.

Uinta River—above the end of the road.

Virgin River—in Zion National Park.

Weber River—Scrambled Egg Bend.

EXPERT

American Fork River.

Big Cottonwood Creek—in canyon down to catch pond.

Ferron Creek—upper.

Fremont River—Torrey to Capitol Reef campground.

Huntington Creek (high water) and Left Fork of Huntington Creek.

Lake Fork—high water.

Logan River—lower canyon at high water.

Ogden River—lower canyon at high water.

Price Canyon—high water.

Provo River—Provo Falls to Cobblerest Campground.

Salina Creek—Pinball section.

San Rafael River—Black Boxes at high water.

Sixth Water.

Snake River—Milner section.

Virgin River—Timpoweap Canyon.

Willow Creek.

TWO RIVER RUNNERS

Much has been written about the early river runners in Utah, especially on the Green and Colorado Rivers. They mainly used larger craft and rowed their boats. In more recent times, two people stand out for their contributions to river running and river preservation. They were both humble men who ran rivers, not to brag, but for the sheer love of adventure in the outdoors, and who made safety an important part of their trips. They not only explored many rivers, but also helped introduce smaller boats, particularly kayaks, to the state.

LES JONES

Leslie A. Jones was born in Montana in 1922 and grew up along the Missouri River, where he had to row across the river every day to get to school. After going to college to become a civil engineer, he moved to Salt Lake City in 1953. That same year, he joined two of his famous river-running relatives, Bus and Don Hatch, in a raft trip through Lodore Canyon on the Green River. The trip was to support the Sierra Club in opposing a dam on the Green River in Dinosaur National Monument. He was hooked on the rivers of Utah and on preserving them.

On this trip he also became aware of the disagreements that crop up on a boat with multiple people. He decided solo boating was the only way to go. Back home, he modified his canoe with aluminum sheeting on the bottom, inserting bulkheads front and back, adding a canvas spray deck, and putting oarlocks on the sides so he could row instead of paddle.

In August of the same year, he made the first solo canoe run of Cataract Canyon. He also made it in record time, leaving Moab at 6 A.M., running some of the biggest whitewater in the state, and arriving at Hite the next day at 6 P.M. He felt that the Big Drops deserved their reputation but considered Dark Canyon Rapid (now under Lake Powell) to be the hardest.

The Cataract trip whetted his appetite for more big water. He decided to tackle the Grand Canyon. He left in November of the same year and ran solo to the Bright Angel bridge. He'd run out of vacation time by then, so he cached his boat and hiked out. He went back in April of 1954 with Bus and Ted Hatch and finished the trip with only one tip-over for the entire canyon.

In 1955, along with Bus and Don Hatch, Les ran the Green and Colorado rivers in one trip from Wyoming to Lake Mead. He then married Katherine Axman. She went with him to run the Middle Fork and Main Salmon in a Grumman canoe to which he'd added oarlocks. By the time they reached Dagger Falls, Les once again had to stop due to work. They cached the boat. Les returned in September to finish the trip solo. He made the 203-mile trip to Riggins in 7 days.

Les went with Allen Neal in 1957 to run the mighty Fraser River in Canada, running at 200,000 to 700,000 cfs. It had never been successfully run between Prince George and Yale. It was so fast that they covered 190 miles in the first two days. They managed to survive huge rapids and monstrous whirlpools as much as 500 feet wide.

Les used his engineering skills to build the only aluminum kayak that I've seen. He may also have built the first keyhole cockpit. He felt it should be easy to exit a kayak. I don't believe Les ever tried to learn to roll. He rarely ever tipped over and ran enough rivers full of logs that he preferred to exit immediately. If he hit a log, he wanted to be able to jump out on top of it before the kayak tipped over.

Many of the smaller rivers in Utah were first done by Les Jones, often in the company of Cal Giddings. Les ran many in the Uinta Mountains, including the Provo, Yellowstone, Uinta, Lake Fork, Rock Creek, Whiterocks, Weber, Bear, Blacks Fork, and Henry's Fork. Most of these were done in the 1970s. He also liked the rivers of south and central Utah, where he ran the Spanish Fork River, Diamond Fork, Sevier, Price, Muddy Creek, Fremont, San Rafael, Virgin, Dolores, and Escalante (first run by Harry Aleson and Georgie White in 1948).

Always concerned about protecting rivers, Les was instrumental in starting American Rivers, a leading river conservation organization. He also helped create the Western River Guides Association in 1958.

Les was an interesting sight on the river. Besides using a homemade aluminum kayak, he always wore a helmet covered with a tin can with a camera mounted on top. He used this to take pictures almost every 50 yards. With all these pictures and with his engineering skills he produced a number of the finest maps made of many western rivers, including the Colorado River through the Grand Canyon, the Green River through Lodore, Desolation, and Gray Canyons, the Middle Fork and Main Salmon, and the Fraser River.

Les mainly ran rivers for the beauty he saw and the friendships he made. He lives close to one of the rivers he loves, the Provo River, and continues to paddle and fight for river protection.

Some of the information on Les was taken from an article by Werner Huck in the March 1995 *Sports Guide*.

CAL GIDDINGS

J. Calvin Giddings was born in September of 1930 in American Fork, Utah. He loved sports and was quite athletic, running track and playing football in high school. He always loved exploring the outdoors and was often taken by his father to prospect in the canyons near his home.

Cal graduated from BYU and then earned his Ph.D. at the University of Utah in 1954. He continued with postdoctoral work at the University of Wisconsin. This is where he actually first started running rivers. He joined a canoe club and ran the Flambeau and Wolf Rivers. He returned to Utah in 1957 to be on the faculty in the Chemistry Department at the University of Utah. He won many awards as a chemist and was world renowned for some of the processes he developed. He authored or co-authored many scientific books and papers.

Cal was involved a great deal in climbing and ski touring. He did several first ascents, including the west face of Lone Peak. He also climbed in the Tetons, Devils Tower, and many local areas. He came to a point in his climbing that he felt that going further was too risky for a family man. Needing a new medium for enjoying the outdoors, he decided to take up kayaking.

During this time, Cal went down the Yampa River on the first-ever Wasatch Mountain Club river trip. He also ran Glen Canyon before it was dammed in 1958. These were both raft trips. He really wanted to kayak, but kayaks just weren't available. When his wife found a mold for a kayak, he built one. He went on his first kayak trip on the Snake River in 1959. He taught himself how to kayak from books and by just getting out and trying. His boat was too wide to roll, but a few years later he came across a mold for a more "modern," narrower kayak. After building his new kayak he eventually taught himself to roll. Since there weren't any other kayakers around, he got his friends to learn.

Cal's love of the outdoors made it natural for him to get involved in the environmental movement. He made the original proposal for the Lone Peak Wilderness Area. He worked with Les Jones in founding the American Rivers Conservation Council (now American Rivers); co-founded Utah's Save Our Rivers Committee; and served as president of both the Wasatch Mountain Club and American Whitewater Affiliation. He started the kayaking division of the Wasatch Mountain Club, started their first conservation committee, and organized pool sessions at the University of Utah.

In 1963, Cal ran part of the Middle Fork of the Salmon with Stu Gardner, another early kayak pioneer. In 1965, Cal led the first descent of Cross Mountain of the Yampa River. This was in a day when helmets weren't used and the kayaks were fiberglass. This was a very challenging run for its time.

In June of 1971, Cal and friends made the first run of the Upper Black Box of the San Rafael River. The next year they ran the Lower Black Box. In between (September of 1971), they made the first run of the South Fork of the Salmon in Idaho. These were all difficult, rugged, and remote gorges.

The most challenging run of his life and another first was in 1975 when he led a group of kayakers down the Apurimac River in Peru, the headwaters and most demanding section of the Amazon River. This adventure is covered in his book *Demon River, Apurimac,* published by the University of Utah Press shortly before his death.

Throughout the 1970s, Cal explored many Utah rivers, often with Les Jones. He was on some of the rivers listed above in the section on Les. In the 1980s, Cal cut back on exploration to spend more time enjoying river running with his family and friends. As rivers became more crowded and the spontaneity was diminished by permits, he looked for other means of getting into the backcountry. He started mountain biking in 1986 with his first ride on the Slickrock Trail near Moab.

Cal enjoyed the dynamic nature of kayaking and river running. He also kayaked to explore the unknown and get into the wilderness. He went on his last exploration into the unknown when he passed on in October of 1996 from cancer.